Saving Sebastian

Saving Sebastian:

A Father's Journey through his Son's Drug Abuse

Dr. Charles Taylor

ISBN 978-0-9827514-5-9
Library of Congress Control Number: 2010940951

Cover Art by Corina Carmona

Manufactured in the United States
Four Genres Press, Jasper, Texas
4genrespress.com
    An imprint of Ink Brush Press

DEDICATION

This book is for fathers—especially for fathers who did not ask to be fathers because they sensed they did not possess the skills needed to be good ones.

May this book bless your struggles, pains, and joys.

"The fathers have eaten sour grapes, and the children's teeth are set on edge."

Ezekiel 18:2

I'm here to write about my son, my second son, the boy who went bad and gave us so much trouble. "Sebastian" I'll call him: Sebastian, who resembles his mother with his striking ivory skin and black hair; Sebastian, the beautiful child, the quiet child, who could play for hours building elaborate skyscrapers and giant battleships with chunks of lumber I'd gotten free at a lumber yard for both my sons to use as blocks.

Sebastian loved our trips from Austin to the Brackenridge Park and the Zoo in San Antonio during spring or autumn when the weather in Texas is perfect. We'd pack a picnic lunch to eat under the ancient live oaks, ride the small red train around the park, and go to see the lions, tigers and giraffes, his favorites. One thing Sebastian always refused to try was the elephant ride, even though his older brother Parker would jump right up on an elephant's back and ride sitting in front of me.

"Come on, Sebastian," I'd yell to him. "You don't want to go through life never having ridden an elephant."

"No," he'd shout back and stamp his feet.

I wrote a poem about our elephant-riding disagreement in ten syllable lines. In poems you have the license to alter facts to get at emotional truth:

> I thought it worth the risk, our lives perhaps,
> to ride the back of the elephant at
> the Brackenridge Zoo. What kind of risk? Less

I guessed than crossing a crowded road. All
your life you'd recall the feel of wrinkled
elephant skin against your sweating hands,
you'd recall the lumbering grey waves of
muscle moving in the animal's back.
All your life, a moving point to return
to, a kind of serene eternity
of the memory--but the boy pushed with
all his small hard might. My son chose to draw
back, his hand secure in his mother's hand.

Here, I've introduced you to my boy, but I don't know exactly how to go about putting down the hard things I will need to say. All I can do, reader, is hack away, hack away—an amateur playing a bad game of golf, hitting the ball but never being sure where it's going to land since a golf ball can slice and curve in all sorts of directions and take on a life of its own.

I'd like for this to be a novel, but novels tend to be a long ride. My fingers might grow weary typing; my wrists could ache, my back throb; I might develop car-

Better to do interior traveling and ride the submarine of words into the soul to make an offering to the world that might shed some light and help make us all a little wiser and better.

pal tunnel syndrome if I set about to write a long novel, which I'd want to do in one big gulp—fast—because I get just six unpaid weeks off in the summer from my teaching job.

You could do so many other great things in six weeks, like hiking the Allegheny Mountain Trail, or like traveling south of the equator to see Venezuela. That country must have something going for it since our so "honest" Republican and Democratic politicians keep bashing its elected president. Venezuela's a small country compared to ours. What are these American politicians so afraid of—that we might have to wean ourselves from our addiction to foreign oil and gain self-sufficiency by developing wind, solar, and tidal power?

I've never been south of the equator and yearn like any soul for adventure, but with the cost of fuel so high these days, well, it's better to sit put, don't you think? Better to do interior traveling and ride the submarine of words into the soul to make an offering to the world that might shed some light and help make us all a little wiser and better, hard at times though the journey may turn out to be in these hard economic times.

So I'll stick close to the novel idea for the time being. I call it a novel because the perceptions presented are mine and mine alone, and they are told in story form. What I am trying to share, however, are events that actually happened, but the fact remains these events are seen through my eyes and no other's. Maybe I should call this work a novel-memoir, a "new" kind of memoir that admits that it can't help but engage unconsciously in some fiction-alizing, since my memory, like any other's, is active, engaged in bias, and always reorganizing information from the past.

You can see I am insecure with what I've undertaken in these six weeks. Can I get away with the "crime" of writing? Life is always throwing you a curve, getting in your face and demanding you fix the leak in the roof or help somebody through rough financial or emotional times. I just bought new clothes for two of my grand-children; they lost nearly everything in an apartment fire. I pulled the carpet out of our bathroom last month because, after the toilet flooded, mold got in the carpet, and, in one night, the smell became like rotting formaldehyde.

I've got a pile of tile sitting in the hallway next to the bathroom waiting for me to cut it and glue it down on the cement. I've got a sack of glue and a special trowel. I even borrowed the tile cutter from my eldest son Parker's girlfriend, but, so far, all this stuff does is sit, get in the way, and gather dust.

Life gets in your face. To write is a crime against practical obligations. It's a crime also because, sure as shootin', some folks are not going to like what you write. Others prefer silence; let the family skeletons stay locked inside a basement vault. Still, I am going to tell you about my wonderful second son Sebastian and his troubled journey.

Right from the time he was a toddler, he had trouble commun-icating. He would get so angry. This was when he was two and three, after he learned to talk, and I would ask, "Are you sad? Are you mad?" And he would stand in the living room of our Austin

3

house on Ravensdale, shake his head, and grow more frustrated. He couldn't find any words to say what he was feeling. Where Sebastian seemed to find most comfort was watching Mr. Rogers on PBS educational television. He really believed, when Mr. Rogers looked directly into the camera and spoke with his soft, intimate voice, "You are special," that the man could see him and was speaking solely to him.

Maybe he didn't want to explain to his father what bothered him. Maybe compared to Mr. Rogers, with my long hair and beard, I looked too big and intimidating. This second child, I figured out many years later, was a secretive kid. He loved fireworks so much he tried to keep a secret stash for himself hidden in the bedroom

> **Maybe he didn't want to explain to his father what bothered him.**

closet. He was crazy about this ice cream shop called "Nothing Strikes Back" on Guadalupe ("the drag"), next to the University of Texas in Austin.

The store was decorated with hippie posters, old marijuana paraphernalia, and black paint on the walls. You sat down at a black table on black chairs lit by ultraviolet lights. Sebastian actually cried one night in 1979 when he was eight and we couldn't find Nothing Strikes Back. We had walked up and down Guadalupe searching closely for the place, but it had closed its doors.

"Change happens," I said to him. "Even ice cream shops are mortal."

2

If I had been perceptive I might have, right then, sniffed out troubles to come.

Sebastian dropped out of school in 1985 when he was fourteen. Well, he didn't exactly drop out. I would drive him to school and walk him to his first class at Austin's Burnet Middle School. Sometime during the day, after I'd left the school for work, he'd walk right out of that school and either his mother or I would get a telephone call that he'd gone truant. Where he went we were never able to determine. Perhaps he and his friends hung out in back alleys, or perhaps they went to the empty home of some friend's working parents. Maybe Sebastian had a hideaway all by himself in some forgotten section of woods along one of Austin's many creeks, such as Waller Creek or Shoal Creek.

> **After I'd left the school for work, he'd walk right out of that school and either his mother or I would get a telephone call that he'd gone truant.**

All this happened before the courts got involved in fining parents when their kids are not in school. Later, I got to know a poor single mother of two teenage boys who was struggling to pay truancy fines. A native of El Salvador, she finally de-enrolled both boys from Austin High and told the school officials she was moving to South Carolina to work in the furniture industry.

She couldn't afford to move, of course, but she did get rid of the fines. I can't see holding a mother who weighs one hundred pounds and is five foot two responsible for two teenage boys who each weigh over a hundred and ninety pounds and stand above six feet. How can she prevent them from slipping out the school's backdoor?

What the courts do is not right, and I think what it's secretly about is getting these kids out of school and into the privatized prison system. That's my radical opinion. Officials in Florida plan the building of new prisons based on the number of students who fail the high school graduation exam. There is much cabbage to be made from taxpayers by companies making big donations to politicians who legislate huge sums for the building and maintenance of prisons operated by private companies. Privately run prisons are one of America's fastest growing industries.

But I'm rambling here. I am writing a novel or maybe a memoir, and both are big houses with wide yards front and back.

3

Maybe we should discuss global warming? My mother, Miriam, was a pioneer ecologist and a member of both the Sierra Club and the Audubon Society. She never wanted to have kids, and on a hot August summer vacation day in Elmhurst, Illinois, when I was fourteen, she sat me down on the living room sofa and explained the views of philosopher Thomas Malthus—all the stuff about the population growing geometrically through the generations on a planet with fixed space and resources. She was a smart woman, a physician with a specialty in anesthesiology.

> "I never should of had kids; your father forced me," my mother said.

I'm not sure I ever got Malthus right.

"I never should of had kids; your father forced me," my mother said. "Now don't you go off and have kids. Don't make the same mistake I made and contribute to overpopulation." She was a charter member of Zero Population Growth. She loved getting out in the remote northern Minnesota woods by a lake—not that far from where she grew up in Minneapolis—to identify birds. She loved solitude and didn't much care for people, my mother Miriam.

Her mother had died giving birth to her, and my mother never talked about that loss. I wonder how it made her feel. She had no mother around to teach her how to be a mother and do all the loving and nurturing mother things, but she did have a wonderful father, my grandfather, a postman who had fought in the Spanish-American war and who later attended the Minneapolis Unitarian Church and became an atheist. Unitarians even then were tolerant of different religious points of view. I consider atheism another religion. Grandfather kept journals and read Darwin and drew pictures of plants he would identify in the Minnesota woods. I never met a man who laughed more than my grandfather, who retired at fifty and lived to be eighty-four.

Ah, but my second son. I often wondered, as I lay on my side of the bed in San Angelo, Texas, across from my pregnant wife, if in the womb he could pick up on my energy. Did he feel my negative vibes? Did he know that I'd been taught from childhood that the planet was in peril due to overpopulation? How did my mother know these things back in the early 1940's? Did she have as wise a professor in her studies at the University of Minnesota as Al Gore had at Harvard in the 1960's? I don't know. I have a small prejudice against Ivy League schools, picked up from my father. He called them second-rate has-beens.

> **Poor Sebastian, poor son. Did he pick up on my hostile vibes as he kicked in his mother's womb?**

Poor Sebastian, poor son. Did he pick up on my hostile vibes as he kicked in his mother's womb? No one should blame the boy. Sebastian did not ask to be born, and I certainly didn't want a child coming into this failing, overheating planet, full of the starving third-world poor and constant warfare, wondering if he had the right to exist. That wasn't right. I had absorbed my mother's teaching well: Don't bring a child into an overpopulated, polluted planet as you were brought into such a place.

4

had to go to therapy to learn I had the right to exist, weekend group therapy sessions held in an old storefront San Angelo building that had been turned into a Unitarian Church. We all sat in a circle on folding chairs. This was in 1972, when Transactional Analysis, or TA, was a magic psychological cure, and its bible, *I'm OK, You're OK*, had come and gone from the best-seller lists. I'm not sure I know today what trans-actional analysis is all a-bout, but I do recall when the sweet, tidy, specially trained nurse who ran the session told our group we had to find the central problem in our psyches that needed work.

> **Self-assertion was not the same as aggression we were told.**

A few of the men in the group were so blocked emotionally the weekend was for them a waste. They never could get down deep enough inside to find out what was troubling them. My wife Eileen, I recall, wanted to learn to be more self-assertive. Self-assertion was not the same as aggression we were told. My wife informed me she was not learning this to act more self-assertive around me; it was to deal with her associates at work (ha, ha).

Eileen had a love for psychology and its latest fads, a devotion perhaps developed in her training as a nurse. She was a loving, trusting person with a sharp mind and a great memory. If Eileen wanted to, I knew she could go far in her profession. Her father had been an honest car salesman, and she'd grown up in a family of six children always short on cash. I believed naively that, growing up with so many children around in struggling circumstances, she wouldn't mind giving up having children of her own.

I had gotten a Ph.D. in English without ever taking a course in psychology and felt superior to Transactional Analysis. I expected to get nothing out of it, but it shook me down to the core of my core. Our group bonded intensely, almost like a small cult cell. The rules were that you could not take any of the secrets revealed in the group outside the group, and once we all left, we were not supposed to have further contact with one another.

Events came back to me during transactional analysis that I'd long forgotten. I recalled being tied to a closed-in bed at Presbyterian Hospital in Chicago when I was six. I had serious asthma, and my father came to see me only every other day while I was locked in the bed cage that made me alternately terrified, lonely, and bored. My mother never showed up.

> **I realized I had never granted myself the right to exist—the first right of all.**

From July into early September, I would go to bed at home every night wondering if I would be alive the next morning, my breathing labored and slow due to constricted lungs. Wallpaper sagged off the ceiling from the menthol-smelling steamer that sat on a hotplate next to my bed.

I cried during our TA sessions, remembering moments when my mother said to my sister and me that she hated kids and had never wanted them. Mom would quote W.C. Fields: "A man who doesn't like children can't be all that bad." I realized I had never granted myself the right to exist—the first right of all.

The nurse said that it was amazing I'd gotten as far as I had, that I'd become a teacher, no less, instead of a serial killer or a drunken sailor. Without granting yourself the right to exist, you're stuck down deep in a sewage hole. Pardon the language, but there is no better term for labeling the situation. The nurse said that my mother was illogical. If I had no right to be using up resources on the planet, what right had she? What was she doing here?"

"Oh, my mother attempted suicide twice," I told the nurse.

"That's awful. I'm sorry," she replied.

"My mother lives right here in San Angelo," I said. "I watch over her. My father divorced her after she tried to kill herself the second time. He pays a substantial alimony even though my sister and I are grown."

5

My poor son Sebastian. Does a soft, insistent voice whisper in his head, questioning his right to exist? Is he down in that sewage hole, barely able to make it through the day? The nurse told me during TA that I had the right to exist as much as any blue jay singing in a tree on a spring morning. I will pause at times, sit in the car with the window rolled down before leaving for work, and listen to the songbirds crafting their poetry. It reminds me of when, in her later years, I took my mother to Lake Nasworthy, east of San Angelo, to enjoy flocks of birds migrating north from Mexico. I still have the binoculars and the bird book she used.

Perhaps seeing the birds at Lake Nasworthy reminded my mother, Miriam, of her childhood in Minneapolis and the family's trips to the northern woods. After her father died, sleeping in my bed one Christmas vacation while he was down visiting from Minnesota, Miriam went into a slow slide. She had no friends in Elmhurst where we lived, except the Holderholfs, who had also lived at Randolph Air Force Base in San Antonio when my father was stationed there in the Army Air Force in the 1940s. The two couples had free time on the base to play bridge late into the night and had been able to take a trip together a thousand miles south to Mexico City. My mother said Mexico City had the most perfect weather in the world.

One afternoon, when I was in York High School in Elmhurst, Miriam threw all the plates and glasses in the kitchen against one wall. Another afternoon, she got all the clothes from the closets and drawers in every room and threw them down the basement stairs, yelling, "I am not your servant." Another time, she stayed in bed for a week, smoking Lucky Strike after Lucky Strike, after a man had come up to the window of her car and criticized her for blocking traffic on a downtown road and not knowing how to parallel park.

I'd come home from school, and she would begin one of her two favorite rants, either of which could go on for hours. One repeated rant was how they ought to drop a bomb on all the blacks in the ghettoes of Chicago. The other favorite was about Jews and how they had hooked noses and controlled the banks of the world. While she shouted and moved around the living room, my sister Karen and I listened quietly, nodding silently, and then, when a break came, we made a hasty retreat to our bedrooms for homework.

Gone were the days when mother used to take us to the Oak Park library to check out books or to the Oak Park Unitarian Church designed by Frank Lloyd Wright. Gone were the times on Christmas mornings when she read carefully and seriously the Gospel of Matthew before we were allowed to open presents. Grandfather had taken my mother and her sister Virginia to the Unitarian Church in Minneapolis all during their childhoods. My grandfather never made prejudicial remarks. In his eighties, on trips

> **My mother had no doubts about her right to exist, no matter how parasitic, lazy, or crazed she behaved.**

down from Minneapolis to our house, he'd joke that, according to the *World Almanac*, if he'd been born black, he'd have more years to live.

My second son probably does not remember visiting my crazy mother Miriam at the San Angelo Geriatric Center where she stayed. We'd go swimming in a tiny, tiled swimming pool they had inside the building, mainly intended for the elderly to float around in and regain muscle tone. It was hard to keep Sebastian and his older brother Parker quiet and contained while visiting my mother. They'd have questions about the screaming coming down the hallways or the sad, mumbling patients sitting in the small lobby.

We'd go outside and sit under the mesquite trees in the bright Texas sun, and the boys would play in the dusty dirt with the pill bugs. What a waste—a woman in her late forties, my mother—the medical doctor who'd graduated from medical school when it was almost impossible for women to get into medical school, sitting around in bed all day in the San Angelo Geriatric Center watching TV. Basketball games were her favorite. She told me once she loved to watch the cute men.

My mother had no doubts about her right to exist, no matter how parasitic, lazy, or crazed she behaved. All those years she stayed in the nursing home, she refused to eat meals in the cafeteria or associate with others in the home and consequently made no friends.

The right to exist—maybe this should be the title of my book.

My son probably doesn't remember when my sister Karen was down from Boston for a visit one Christmas vacation and my sister remarked about my mother's taxes and mother grabbed a cola bottle with both hands and swung it over and down at Karen's head. I got my hand up and knocked the bottle aside so it shattered on the floor before it reached my sister's head.

The right to exist—maybe that should be the title of this book. My mother said humans were multiplying like the English rodent lemmings. If she were still around, she'd say global warming is our own rodent march to the sea, our tumbling over the cliff and drowning. Under population pressures, we will behave in certain odd and destructive ways to bring our numbers down and bring balance back to the planet. Maybe that's what we're doing driving the large, gas guzzling SUVs and Hummers: bringing down our own numbers, like lemmings marching to the sea.

6

So my son Sebastian quit going to school, and in the fall of 1987, at the age of sixteen, he moved out of his mother's Austin house—moved into a one-room, closet-sized apartment four blocks west of the University of Texas with another boy about his age He told his mother he had nothing against her; he just needed to be on his own. I visited him shortly after he moved. I needed to store a folding chair, a folding table, and a box of books I was going to try to sell

> **I have always lived my life in a form of idealistic denial.**

from my small press at an open market on a side street across from the University of Texas. My "need" gave me the opportunity to check on my boy.

I set up my table and sat most of the day, selling just two books to a co-ed who I believe felt sorry for me. It was a crystal, cool, beautiful day, a day to enjoy sitting outside, but after a while, one of the open market jewelers turned me in to the police. An officer arrived in a lovely blue uniform looking like a Blue Meanie right out of the Beatles' *Yellow Submarine* and asked to see my permit. I had no permit. The permits cost a couple hundred dollars, and I wanted to find out if there indeed existed customers out there for my books before shelling out the money for a permit.

I hauled the equipment back to my son's tiny room. I'd need to borrow a car to get the stuff back to the bookstore downtown where we lived in the basement. My son seemed a little spacey and not too friendly when I brought back my stuff, but I couldn't say for certain he was on drugs. I have always lived my life in a form of idealistic denial. I was an artist and intellectual dedicated to a revolutionary change in consciousness and thus revolutionary peaceful change in the world. My children would also become artists and intellectuals and be too above-the-crowd to turn to drugs.

I remember how shocked I was to learn that Sebastian, at thirteen, was smoking cigarettes. I figured he'd be too smart and independent to be swayed either by peer pressure or corporate marketing. I walked in an Austin laundromat on 29th street where he was hanging out with Dusty and Harlan, two of his stepbrothers, while they did their laundry, and when my son saw me coming through the glass doors, he stuck the lit cigarette in his back pocket.

I was too shocked to get angry. The son of a professor, the son of an intellectual, he'd heard me speak of the health dangers of smoking at least fifty times. I didn't smoke cigarettes; his mother didn't smoke cigarettes. His two older stepbrothers, however, did smoke cigarettes, and he foolishly idolized them.

7

How could a son of mine become a drug addict? I've carried the grief, the pain, and the guilt about what happened for over twenty years. The gears in my brain have churned many a day and night while I tried to carry through with the normal tasks of living a life and earning a living. Yes, the brain churned, trying to figure out what went wrong, what I did wrong.

You could say—one might say—it was the influence of the stepchildren. That's how it happened. Or you could say it was the influence of my second wife. Courtney had done oodles of LSD in the late 1960s and still was a daily user of marijuana. She loved to talk of the LSD days, how the drug cured her of certain sexual hang-ups (ones she never explained in detail), and how it also opened her mind to spirituality.

> **She loved to talk of the LSD days, how the drug cured her of certain sexual hang-ups (ones she never explained in detail)....**

Courtney had married, at eighteen, a Korean War veteran of thirty and had her first son, Dusty, when she was nineteen. She's been through as many identities as some men go through suits in a lifetime. She'd been a trophy-winning sports car driver, an actress in dinner theatre, a fundamentalist Christian stay-at-home total mom, a seamstress, a writer, and a radical hippie—all while working on a BA and then an MA in English. Her changeability I attributed to her upbringing as a military brat. She attended something like five high schools and spent her early childhood in Germany.

I thought when I married her that we were both going to be creative writers and professors. She got a fellowship to the Ph.D. program in creative writing at the University of Utah, but after two years she abandoned that goal without any clear alternative plan except to return to her grandparents' tiny east Texas hometown, buy a house, and write for a year.

The LSD trips during her hippie period were not always transcendental. One special day she was supposed to spend with her sharecropper grandfather in Canton, in East Texas. She loved him deeply, but she got too ripped and spent the day on a bad trip, staring at the TV on a motel room bed.

Courtney told her children, and anyone else willing to listen, to stick to what was natural—the plants: marijuana, untreated tobacco, or certain mushrooms. If they did that, they couldn't go wrong. Nature was good. She was a fervent neo-pagan while we were married and believed God was nature, and nature was benevolent.

I tried to explain to Courtney that her view of nature was naïve. Oleander, in spite of its beautiful scarlet flowers, has leaves so poisonous that they can kill a child who eats them. The white berries from the mythical mistletoe plant that grows parasitically on trees and that one might hold over a girl's head to steal a kiss are deadly poisonous. I knew of a rancher who made chili with the berries to get rid of his wife. He was tired of tending cattle and dreamed of selling the ranch and moving to San Antonio. His wife had inherited the ranch from her family. Fortunately, the woman took one look at the chili and grew suspicious. She called the cops, and the husband went to jail for attempted murder. But of course my stories of poisonous nature didn't change Courtney's beliefs. Only time and a stroke changed them. Courtney is now a Catholic.

8

Only once did my second wife's two grown sons get my older son Parker, then in high school, to try a joint of marijuana. Many users of the herb become evangelists of the high, which they perceive either as a religious experience or as a great kick. The experiment happened down in the basement of the bookstore we ran in downtown Austin, in 1985, when Parker was a high school sophomore.

Parker became intensely nervous and could not sit still. He paced from one end of the 1,500 square foot basement space to the other. I didn't know that Dusty and Harlan were trying to sell him on the virtues of the herb until I saw him so strung out. He'd had a reverse reaction. Most people turn "mellow" or "laid-back" on marijuana. Time slows down. They lose much of their forward motion and ambition.

> **Many users of the herb become evangelists of the high, which they perceive either as a religious experience or as a great kick.**

Music—playing the viola, piano, and guitar—saved my older son Parker from drugs, I believe. He had such a passion for playing, and he was so talented he convinced a professor of viola to give him free lessons once a week in the music school of the University of Texas. My son and I agree that a life without a passion—something you must do in the world—would be a mean-

21

ingless life. We've often talked about how living for family, living for raising children, is not enough, for us, to give life meaning.

Parker is an intellectual; Parker is an artist. I expected my two blood children and even my three stepchildren all to become artists and intellectuals: painters, sculptors, potters, actors, musicians, or something else. What other way was there to live beautifully and ethically in the world, to make a difference in others' lives and not become enslaved to the dominant wage-slave paradigms? What other way was there to live that could bring such freedom and sensuous happiness? Art teaches you courage, and, contrary to what many believe, art teaches common sense. A person who loves the arts has a place to celebrate dreams and is not going to confuse dreams with reality.

> **Art teaches you courage, and, contrary to what many believe, art teaches common sense.**

Ah, but I was a fool. Only Parker became an artist. He's forty now and quite famous in central Texas as a musician, but he owns next to nothing and still has trouble, at times, making the rent and paying his utility bills, yet he loves what he is doing. He has his passion, and so he is blessed.

9

When I came back on vacation to Austin from my teaching job in Japan in 1991, I would visit my son Sebastian at the Travis County jail. Visiting a child in jail turns out to be a greater dehumanizing experience than one might suppose. We're taxpayers and expect, since we're footing the bill, to be treated with a modicum of decency, but even in our individualistic country, the law seems to want the family to feel collectively responsible. In Travis County in 1991, I entered the jail building into a small vestibule whose walls were painted an army green. There was no place to sit down to wait.

At the appointed time a guard unlocked a windowless metal door, and you followed him into a dirty elevator and up to the second floor. There, you'd find stools to sit on— attached to the floor close to a

> **Visiting a child in jail turns out to be a greater dehumanizing experience than one might suppose.**

wall of thick glass with thin wires crosshatched through it. You had a small ledge to lean your arms on and a phone you could use to talk to your incarcerated loved one. I'm still surprised the phone was not a pay phone.

I tried without success to take pride in the fact my son was a "trustee" in the Travis County jail. He got up early and pushed a cart around delivering food to the other prisoners. He picked up the dirty plates that the prisoners stuck back through the jail door slots and, if requested, brought them old magazines and paperbacks to read.

I never asked Sebastian why he was in the county jail. Was it drugs? Was it because he was living on the streets?

I had always romanticized the life of the great folk activist musician Woody Guthrie and his riding the rails. I'd read a book by an anthropology student called *Rolling Nowhere* that was based on field research riding the rails across the United States for a Master's thesis. On TV I saw an interview with a wealthy man who owned his own large company. As a youth he'd ridden the rails, and every spring his family had to tolerate his intolerable, incurable itch, his vanishing act when he'd hit the rails for five months.

> Is it possible that by some off-the-wall magic, our loved ones live out our unrealized fantasies?

Is it possible that by some off-the-wall magic, our loved ones live out our unrealized fantasies? Courtney, my second former wife, ended up homeless on the streets of Austin in the mid 1990s, four or five years after I'd divorced her. My son Sebastian ended up living on the streets. The closest I came to living on the streets was sleeping for a month or two in the back of a couple of station wagons I owned and living in the woods in a tent along Barton Creek. These were chosen experiments in living, however. They were attempts to find out what the bare-bone necessities were and how to maximize freedom and minimize unpleasant work. I could have stayed at many a friend's house if I had actually been truly down and out.

10

Sebastian and I had never had much to discuss. When he was eleven, in 1982, I used to walk over to his mother's house from our used bookstore in downtown Austin at Fourth and Lavaca.

I walked five miles from downtown to the lovely green central residential district where they lived

> **What does an intellectual say to an eleven-year old boy?**

east of the University. I always enjoyed the exercise from the walk over. Sebastian and I would spend Wednesday evenings together, but we could never think of anything to talk about.

What does an intellectual say to an eleven-year old boy? "Sebastian, ah, do you know why Marx and communism failed?" "Sebastian, I've got this great book of poetry I picked up at the store by Robert Bly. He writes about the mystical light around the body. You may not understand many of the poems but you might enjoy the sounds and get a sense of how sacred the human body is."

And Sebastian, what does he say? Not much. We sit in a small side room near the stairs to the basement and both watch television. When I came on Wednesdays, we always ended up in that small room watching television. Sometimes it was the PBS music show Austin City Limits. Parker would stick his head in the room and say hello, but he was busy practicing his viola and doing homework. I already sensed my son Sebastian had a secret life, a place he loved to go to be by himself or be with friends.

11

To have something to talk about while we stared at each other through the wire glass at the county jail, I told Sebastian I was writing a small book called *How to Be Homeless, or How to Get out of It*. I needed his input to make the book good. Could I ask him questions?

Over the phone, Sebastian told me one of the tricks the homeless use when desperate for money. You wander around a Wal-Mart parking lot until you find a dropped receipt. Then you go in the store and locate the item on the shelf. Next, you take the item up to the return counter, show the receipt, and say you want to return the item. "I'm sorry I forgot the plastic bag," you add.

As long as Sebastian's clothes looked presentable and he didn't look raggedly homeless, he'd get the cost of the item in cash.

Of course, receipts usually had more than one purchase on them. You wanted to pick one item off the receipt that cost a fair amount, but nothing like a hundred dollars. You needed some vague excuse why you were returning the item, such as your spouse did not like it. You

> **The other thing Sebastian told me was how you had to prepare for sleeping on the ground at night.**

couldn't say that you're returning a bag of dog food because your dog died. Well, a person might get away with that excuse with charm and good looks, but doesn't such an excuse, Sebastian explained, sound unbelievable?

The other thing Sebastian told me was how you had to prepare for sleeping on the ground at night. Before you could put your sleeping bags or blankets down, you needed four to five cans of bug spray, and you needed to spray under and out from your sleeping spot heavily to keep the fire ants from attacking in

> **Those first two times, I could not bring myself to believe my own son was stealing.**

the middle of the night. I can remember fire ants getting in one of my station wagons and making a small nest under the seat. One night they attacked me as I slept with the back seat folded down, and I had to drive to an Albertson's all-night supermarket to get the spray to kill them all.

It took all my will power to get up to the county jail to see Sebastian. I was so disappointed in him. School had never been easy for me. As a small child I had always been at the bottom of the class, Mr. Dunce from the first grade on. I had, and still have, low self-esteem, yet I stuck it out. Why couldn't he? Anyone can deal with low self-esteem, and who doesn't have it? You just put your mind on other things.

Sebastian's mother, Eileen, had sent me literature while I lived in Japan: papers on "the enabling parent," "the need to hit bottom," and "tough love." These pop psychology and academic writings confirmed my previous instincts. I had felt so guilty because I had kicked my son out of my house when I found him stealing to support his habit. Not the first couple of times. The first time was when Sebastian went through my stamp collection and sold the most valuable stamps to a stamp dealer. The second happened when he stole all the money I'd hid in an old cabinet at the bookstore from working all day on my feet at a record convention down at Austin's Lady Bird Lake. Those first two times, I could not bring myself to believe my own son was stealing.

12

Sebastian had a friend named Billy, a tall, thin boy with sandy blond hair. They played in a rock band together that practiced in the basement of his mother's house. When Sebastian was sent to county jail again at twenty, he was married to Rachael. Rachael would lay in bed all day, depressed, while Sebastian worked as a waiter out at the Lakeway Country Club fifty hours a week. She was depressed because her father was a poor Southern male and an alcoholic. She'd send me poems in the mail about her father—raw, angry artistic expressions that I admired. One great thing my former wife Eileen accomplished was convincing Sebastian and Rachael to use birth control and not have kids. I can't imagine what his child support payments would be if he had to pay for kids by two former wives. He already pays over seven thousand a year to one former wife.

> I figured Sebastian and Rachael wanted cash to buy drugs, so instead of handing over cash, I brought them a couple of sacks of basic staple groceries

I visited Rachael and Sebastian's apartment at times when they claimed they had no money. I have little initial sympathy for women who stay at home without children and live off their husbands. I figured Sebastian and Rachael wanted cash to buy drugs, so instead of handing over cash, I brought them a couple of sacks of basic staple groceries, like bread and milk and eggs.

Rachael was always in bed in their little efficiency apartment, with stacks of library books scattered on the floor, some of them related to feminism, a lot of them poetry and fiction books. Dishes filled the small kitchenette, in some spots piled up two feet, and the floor of the apartment was covered completely with dirty clothes. I got the feeling Rachael had a thing for older men and was coming on to me because she always came to the door in long, semi-see-through pajamas, and her top would be unbuttoned.

Sebastian's best buddy from the band he'd been playing bass for, sandy-haired Billy, began an affair with Rachael while Sebastian was in jail.

Rachael and Sebastian had met at an alternative high school on Congress in downtown Austin where all the students worked on computers. We were so happy when we convinced Sebastian to return to school, and pleased that the program would take him in even though he

> **Most students spent half the day out back smoking joints.**

had not completed junior high. Billy also attended the school. Everything was done on computers, and they only had a few facilitators who would come over—if you could find one—to explain things when you got stuck.

Sebastian explained that the education was self-paced, and most students spent half the day out back smoking joints. Rachael was a thin redhead who was six-foot-one, a good two inches taller than Sebastian. I bumped into her years later; she was working as a cashier in an Austin gas station/convenience store.

"Sebastian got his GED," I told her. "Did you get yours?"

"Yes," she said. The way her eyes looked over my shoulder suggested she was lying.

"How is your father doing?"

"He died. Two years ago. Sclerosis of the liver." She turned her head and looking away, out the front window.

"I'm sorry." I put my change in my wallet and went out the door. I had once spent a day with her father and mother in the country town of Buda, south of Austin. At that time her father was a truck driver. He did seem a conflicted, unhappy man. Walking back to my car, I remembered my son's wedding day on a Saturday morning in Woldridge Park, across from the old Austin Public Library. In the middle of the park is a cozy old Gazebo where the ceremony took place. Rachael looked stunning—so tall in her flowing white wedding gown and flaming red hair. Sebastian looked great also in his tuxedo, the black of his tux and hair contrasting with his alabaster skin. They were nineteen when they got married. The year was 1990. Two children from chaotic worlds reaching for the convention and structure I'd always distrusted--reaching, perhaps, because of the disorder they felt within. Her father had been there—her shy father—to give his daughter away as a bride.

13

Rachael was actually involved with two men while Sebastian was in jail. The men were fiercely jealous of each other, and Billy happened to see the other guy, Joel, pull his pickup in front of Rachael's place on a rainy afternoon. Billy got a pistol out of his backpack and went out the front door.

> **They shot each other in the front yard in the rain. Joel was killed.**

Joel saw the car of his rival in the driveway. Sebastian had purchased the duplex in part with the inheritance money he'd received from his grandfather, my father. The arriving boy picked up his gun from under the pickup's seat.

They shot each other in the front yard in the rain. Joel was killed. Billy, who had been inside with Rachael, was wounded in the leg. Rachael told the jury that Billy had fired in self-defense, so he got off with a year in jail. No murder charges were filed.

Sebastian and I didn't talk about this when I went to visit him in county jail. I didn't know how much he knew about what his wife was doing, or even if she was visiting him. I had divorced my second wife, Courtney, in 1991 for reasons too complicated to go into here and moved to Japan to teach for Texas A&M University at a campus they opened in the city of Koriyama. Sebastian never wrote me while I was in Japan, nor did his brother. I came home twice a year, eager to see them both, but both boys were adults by then, working and married with their own lives. They did not have much time for a father who had left them when they were six and four. I considered my father an absent father because he worked five and a half days a week and commuted eight hours a week to and from work.

What kind of absent father was I? A worse one. No question.

I've been to jail myself a couple of times: twice for outstanding traffic tickets and once for protesting clear cutting in the Sam Houston National Forest by chaining myself to a tree. I often blame my second wife and her children for corrupting my son, but what about me?

> **What kind of absent father was I? A worse one. No question.**

I can't forget, either, that my former wife Eileen was smoking pot and doing LSD for years with her boyfriend Mack after we split up.

I understand now that Sebastian had no respect for his father —no respect and some hatred—because I had left his mother and abandoned him and his brother. Not only had I abandoned them, but I had also stopped paying child support. I quit paying support because my former wife and I had agreed to share the children equally—six months of each year at each of our residencies—but then my former wife reversed herself. The sharing agreement we had worked out personally after our divorce was purely verbal. The earlier legal divorce decree gave her custody with visitation rights for me.

In the divorce settlement Eileen got the suburban house that we'd rented out in Austin north of the airport. Austin real estate was booming, and when she sold the house in 1976, she made a twenty-three thousand dollar profit.

I felt that was plenty enough money.

14

I drifted deeper into the Bohemian artist life after I got together with my second wife Courtney. We had little money, ever. We usually had no car, and we slept for many years in the basement of the used bookstore we managed. I made four hundred a month; she made four hundred a month. The truth is I was glad to be away from my kids because, like my mother, I had not wanted kids and had always wanted a life of adventure and freedom. My second spouse, Courtney, had three kids, but the oldest was a teenage boy who was glad, for a small fee, to do baby-sitting.

Yet at times, I would experience such pain and longing for my children.

Courtney and I went out nights in downtown Austin and had a great time going to plays and art openings and sitting talking in bagel shops and bars. She was a writer/intellectual with ideas not the same but similar to mine. In our outlooks, Courtney was more hippie, and I was more New Left. We thought we could work out a way to save the planet from disaster; we were so much in love and learning so much from each other. Many books I never had to read because she told me all about them.

She admired Flannery O'Conner as a short story writer but argued that O'Conner's vision was limited because Flannery never had children. The first couple of years we were together, I believed our conversations sparkled with such unfettered brilliance they should have been taped for posterity.

Yet at times, I would experience such pain and longing for my children. I recall reading in D.H. Lawrence how it used to drive the novelist crazy when his wife Frieda would get deep into the same kind of longing. I missed my first wife, too, but I saw her as the great betrayer, the

> **and then, once the presence of the children made me fall in love with them, she took them away**

woman who got herself pregnant after agreeing to a marriage with no children and then, once the presence of the children made me fall in love with them, had taken them away to a different city. We had been living in El Paso when we divorced in 1976; in a few months, she packed up a U-Haul with her new lover, Mack, and moved to Austin.

Mack resembled me. He was tall, thin, and had a beard, but he was much more handsome, with a craggy face, intense blue eyes, and jet-black hair.

Does Sebastian know any of this history?

Probably not.

Would he care and believe me?

It's too late.

What he finds significant is that I left.

I have never tried to discuss the terrible traumas he went through. He continues to love his mother deeply. She was always there for him and continues to be there for him, at times loaning him money he does not pay back. I never could bring myself to say anything critical of her.

So there that poor boy was, only four years old. We were living in an apartment complex in west El Paso, and one night, without warning, his father did not come home. I found myself driving back and forth on the I-10 through town till three in the morning and finally went to stay at the apartment of a gay woman friend of mine to sort things out.

Always there'd been a powerful emotional connection between Sebastian and me. I stayed at home a year in 1973/4 as a house husband. We'd spent many afternoons fishing on a creek close to the old Austin airport and other afternoons at a Bartholomew park with its large swimming pool. Sebastian was always trying to compete with his older brother Parker in our various activities, and he could not do it. He'd come to me in tears after, say, a game of croquet he'd lost in the front yard. I'd try to explain to him, "You're two years younger. Wait till you grow up. Then you'll be able to beat him at things."

That was cold comfort for a three-year-old who considered himself inferior. I had prayed that our second child be born a girl to avoid damaging compet-

> **I know the one year I stayed home with the boys was one of the best of my life.**

itiveness, having seen what it had done to cousins of mine. These days, girls compete with their older brothers as much as they would with an older sister. Still, I know the one year I stayed home with the boys was one of the best of my life. I never much liked working for a living and got to feel close to them in a way I had never felt before. All fathers should have the opportunity to spend at least one year at home taking care of and bonding with their children.

15

Ah, Sebastian. There are so many blank holes in our history. There were so many years apart. I did not telephone because telephone calls were expensive before the breakup of the ATT and GTE phone monopolies. Courtney and I had little money. We often were too poor even to afford a phone in the house. I don't believe I wrote letters that often, either. I never remembered your birthday. It's in April, is it not? Here, I've forgotten again.

I do remember in 1971 dropping your mother off at Shannon Hospital in San Angelo, and then going back to campus at Angelo State to teach my survey American literature class. A student

> **Being unhappy about the birth of a child was, back then, a totally unacceptable emotion.**

worker with a big smile came into the class and gave me a folded sheet of paper that said you had been born. When I told the class of your birth, they were stunned that I'd even come to class.

They did not know how unhappy I was about your birth. Being unhappy about the birth of a child was, back then, a totally unacceptable emotion. No one ever dared to admit to such feelings (except my mother to her own children at home). I tried to edit the feelings out of my heart and act like a proud and happy new daddy. I bought cigars and gave them to my colleagues at work. Underneath, I felt even more the work slave, trapped in the middle of nowhere out in San Angelo in remote, mostly empty West Texas, in a town that seemed owned and run by right-wing Christians I could not relate to.

The dream I thought we shared, Eileen and I, of both working part-time and living in San Francisco, had turned out to be an illusion. Even today I think about how, if the two of us had moved to San Francisco in 1969 when I finished the coursework for my Ph.D., I could have become allied with the beat movement in literature, and we'd be millionaires now because we'd have bought a house that would have inflated by the year 2000 to fifty times its original value. Fortunately, I have been able to teach Beat American writers in classes and develop friendships with some still alive.

> **I wonder if either Sebastian or his brother recalls when I tried to get them to stop wetting their beds by positive reinforcement.**

Ah, but I tried not to hold any of this against you, Sebastian. You were an easy child to care for, compared to your older brother. You did not suffer from terrible colic as Parker had, and you quickly got on a regular schedule of waking and sleeping through the night. If I told Parker not to touch the stove because it was hot, he'd test me, but if I said not to put the fork in the wall socket because it would give you a terrible shock, you handed me the fork to put away. What a sweet and easy-going child you were, a joy to be around.

I wonder if either Sebastian or his brother recalls when I tried to get them to stop wetting their beds by positive reinforcement. We were living in a tract house north of the airport on Ravensdale Drive in Austin then. It was 1974. I'm sure they remember that humble place with the garden we planted out back, the two mimosa trees in the front yard, and the lung cancer asbestos shingle siding.

I was staying at home to be not only a house husband but also a freelance writer. Mostly I was trying my hand at writing poetry. I had not yet figured out there was no money in poetry, and barely a readership either. You two boys would piss in your sleep every night, and the whole bedroom reeked of the odor. So what I did, for positive reinforcement, was to put a poster board chart on the wall. If you boys went five days without urinating in your sleep, I'd buy you each a chocolate Sunday.

But it never worked. One morning, after finding both of your beds wet with urine, I got furious and ripped up the poster with its few gold stars for non-piss nights. I was always having these flare-ups of intense anger. I'd give the boys smacks on the bottoms for this and for that—I don't remember what. I had a reason at the time, perhaps a half-good reason. I remember Parker tearing open the bottom of his new blue jeans sliding down a hill after I'd warned him and given him cardboard to slide down on, but underneath was this profound resentment, this anger that my dreams and my life were being stolen from me. Today, I can see these resentments as immature, but I was a young man then and had known for a long time I was not proper father material.

> I was always trying to control, to hide that anger, but it would break out.

So these children had ruined my life, my destiny to be a writer and poet, by taking San Francisco away and exiling me to right-wing Texas. The great songwriter Bob Dylan said that destinies are fragile things, and one should never announce them in the world because the jealous and the more conventional, those whose horizons are limited by society's roles, will despise those with dreams and try to defeat them. I wish I'd had the perceptivity of Bob Dylan; I wish I'd had his distrust of the human race.

I was always trying to control, to hide that anger, but it would break out. It was not their fault. Children are innocent, yet they fall into the history of others. Let me kill, by control and by will, my disappointment, my regret, my despair, and my anger—at being tricked and betrayed, at having my dream stolen from me. It would have been different if, from my own foolishness or moral errors, I had lost my dream, but I trusted my spouse, and we both worked so hard getting educations for the dream I believed we shared.

People are so varied. Not long ago I listened to a young woman cry in a creative writing workshop on memoirs I was taking in Austin's Resistencia Bookstore. She was holding a small photo of her baby hooked up to a machine in the hospital. She and her husband had gone to various fertility clinics trying to have a child, and after six years they'd finally had a baby, but the child had died in six months. The woman was angry with God for taking her child, angry at God for denying her a child when so many people had babies they did not want. Finally she said she was thankful to God for giving her the child for the short six months.

16

Ah, but all justification or rationalization aside—to have abandoned two young children, years four and six, to have abandoned a wife of twelve years, suddenly and without any discussion or warning, to have not come home one night, and then to have moved quickly in with another woman!

No wonder the second son disliked me. He sees what I did as a highly immoral and irresponsible act. I see it as an act of a man with a deficient soul approaching the suicidal and attempting to rescue himself. I see it as an act of a man lashing out at a life that seemed too demanding — long hours of work in an academic career preparing classes, grading papers, attending committee meetings—and worst of all, competing with others by publishing scholarly papers for tenure and promotion. What was that all about? I wanted to be friends with my colleagues. I wanted to be out in the world doing adventurous things and writing poems and novels about those things, not sitting at a desk in a small office room at a college day after day.

> **All those car payments and mortgage payments and trips to the pediatrician weighed on me.**

All those car payments and mortgage payments and trips to the pediatrician weighed on me, as did the thought of twenty years back and forth, back and forth, commuting to this office or that in order to be a womb slave, to keep a woman happy by providing the money for raising children. Eileen was pressing me to buy a house in El Paso, pressing me to let her quit her nursing job so she could be a full-time, stay-at-home mother, and pressing me to adopt a third child. We even went to an interview with an adoption counselor. We told the woman we did not care what race the child was.

It seemed overwhelming, boring, and soulless, that middle class life. You can say I was lacking in love and lacking in a sense of responsibility for not jumping at the chance to clamp on that white collar and hook up that leash of a tie. You could call me all sorts of names, or you might say, well, look, he was twenty when he got married. A twenty-year-old man has a right to refuse to be a parent. A twenty-year-old man is a wise man if he knows he lacks the skills to be a parent and tells a woman frankly he does not think he will ever acquire the skills. There is no law on God's good earth that says a man must have children. If a woman doesn't like the arrangement, she can go ahead and marry someone else. Studies indicate that couples married a long time say the happiest periods were before children and after children grew up. The best marriage I know is between a librarian and a former grade school principal. She was twenty years younger than he, but they'd always been happy—and childless.

> **You will find a few blank pages at the back of this book to rant as I am doing here. . . .**

You will find a few blank pages at the back of this book to rant as I am doing here—that is, if you wish. And that's fine with me. I don't care. I've come to terms with what I did. I made efforts to spend time with Sebastian, but if he needs to dislike me for who I happen to be—a highly reluctant father—then let him go ahead. He is a free adult now, at liberty to make his own judgments and work out his own choices.

17

Sebastian shared with me one time, in the summer of 1991, where he and his homeless buddies used to sleep. It was a ledge in a huge cement culvert behind Bookpeople in Austin at the Brodie Oaks Shopping Center near Ben White and Lamar. This was the time when his mother wouldn't let Sebastian in her house or give him money. This was tough love time.

> **He was living with a stripper named Kelly who had bailed him out of the county jail.**

"Yeah, the police knew we all were there but left us alone. We could gather wood and build a fire to keep warm through the winter nights."

There was a slight pride in his voice. He knew I had tendencies to glamorize hobo life.

"I also had a camp off Airport Boulevard behind Lammes Candies, back in the woods. I'd built a shack out of scavenged plywood and cardboard. One time the cops found me and told me to clear out. I didn't argue with them. I just packed a few belongings and left."

"That must have been hard," I said. "Did the place keep the rain off?"

"Yeah, it did—most of it. I moved back in the next day and never saw the cops again."

Sebastian laughed and shook his head. He'd developed a dry, if rueful, sense of understated humor.

When he was telling me of his old outdoor living spots, he was living with a stripper named Kelly who had bailed him out of the county jail. The stripper looked a bit too short to be highly successful in a tough business. She was a stocky young woman, but she did have an impressive rack, and they were all hers—no silicone--it seemed to me, from the way they moved under her shirt. I never saw her perform. Strip joints always seemed to me pathetic places for losers, sad men willing to throw away large sums on nothing, not even any honest touch, because for some heartrending reason they were unable to find a woman to love.

Kelly lived in an apartment close to MLK Boulevard with an understanding boyfriend and performed at Austin's Yellow Rose on north Lamar. Sebastian felt a strong attachment to this lady for rescuing him. Her mother was always calling from Michigan and telling her to get out of the strip club business, where women often resort to

> **Many years later Sebastian told me that both Kelly and her boyfriend were heroin users.**

taking speed to keep their energy up and their weight down. Many years later Sebastian told me that both Kelly and her boyfriend were heroin users. I had noticed nothing unusual, and it never occurred to me.

"Maybe you should think about what your mother says," Sebastian told her once when I was visiting. Sebastian introduced me, when I first came by to visit him, as a professor at Texas A&M. That wasn't exactly true. I was a lecturer overseas at an A&M extension campus in Japan. He told all his friends I was a professor, and that seemed the one thing about his father that made him proud. I wondered if he ever thought of my love for art and writing, or of the energy and sacrifice I put into writing my books and publishing other writers' books through my publishing firm. I wondered if it ever crossed his mind that art was divine to me, a passionate spirituality.

I certainly never told him. How do you speak of such things without sounding idiotic?

18

Sebastian finally did hit bottom, reaching that last place where he realized no one would rescue him, and he would have to rescue himself. The whole experience was one of the scariest periods of our lives. Would he hit bottom and be squashed dead, or would he somehow bounce and turn his life around? My former wife Eileen and I had no way of knowing. We lived in constant nail-biting worry.

> **Sebastian was holding down a job, but he seemed about to drink himself to death.**

The months we waited put us in a wailing place where all we wanted to do was tear hair out.

The turn upwards came when he got a job as a cook at Waterloo Ice House in Austin near the corner of 6th and Lamar early in 1992. Months went by. He had pulled himself together enough to hold a job. When I returned from Japan for a visit six months later near Christmas, I climbed those lovely old dark wooden stairs to his upstairs apartment behind Austin Community College on Rio Grande so hopefully; then he opened the door to usher me in, and there were beer cans everywhere, empty beer cans standing like trolls with their hands behind their backs all over the floor, along the window sills, on all the kitchen counters, behind the toilet in the bathroom, around the tub. They were everywhere, and the amazing thing was they were all empty. What kept him from carrying the empty cans to the trash as he headed to the refrigerator to get another? I saw it as a bizarre shrine to the god of BEER. Sebastian was holding down a job, but he seemed about to drink himself to death.

"What are you doing?" I said to him. "Don't you know that both your grandfathers were alcoholics? You've inherited the genes of alcoholics."

"It's a phase I'm going through." He laughed, looking away. "You know, youthful rebellion."

We were headed out the door, over to his mother's apartment right next door, for some kind of family reunion. Eileen's mother and two sisters were in town. Eileen had rented her house out and separated from her long-time lover Harrel. When she left, Harrel ripped her favorite original Sarah Byrd oil off the wall and threw it in the trash. Eileen had taken the apartment next to her son in this lovely old building near Lamar to keep an eye on him.

Sebastian worked his way up to a position of fair responsibility, kitchen manager, before he quit Waterloo Ice House where his older brother played music with his jazz band once a week. He quit to work as a flower salesman under tents that had become the rage around the state for selling flowers at lower prices than brick and mortar florist shops. The pay, he said, was better, but I suspected the flowers were a cover for selling drugs. When I made my second trip back from Japan for the year in the summer of 1993, he and his salesman buddy from the flower tent were looking for an apartment together.

> It was a scam to get money out of me to buy drugs.

I was making good money in Japan—for me, anyway—and offered to help with the deposit and first month's rent. Sebastian and I went to look at the place, a backyard apartment above an old wooden garage behind a raggedy old white frame house on a big lot close to North Loop. The apartment was typical of a funky Austin neighborhood.

Sebastian's friend was already there and had moved in. That made me suspicious, and the friend picked up on my vibes. He was a young man like Sebastian but his ragged face made him look in his forties.

"We don't need deposit money after all," the friend said. "I got it together. Sebastian needs his side of the rent."

Sebastian gave the guy a dirty look. This meant they were going to get half of what Sebastian had asked for. I suspected Sebastian had no intention of moving in; it was a scam to get money out of me to buy drugs.

I never again heard about the place, or the guy Sebastian supposedly planned to live with. Sebastian was not living with him the next time I returned from Japan.

19

How long had my second son been divorced from his first wife, Rachael? About two years. I had helped the two of them move in and share a duplex with my stepson Harlan out on the Colorado River west of Austin in the River Bend Community. It had been close to where Sebastian was working then as a waiter at a country club. The duplex at River Bend saved him an hour's commute back and forth and about thirty dollars a week on gas, but the living arrangement did not last for long. Harlan, my second stepson, said that Sebastian and Rachael would get into long, drunken, knock-down battles where they would roll around on the floor.

> **One thing was certain: both couples were drinking heavily.**

Sebastian and Rachael said that Harlan and his wife Cynthia would get into knockout fights and roll around on the floor.

Who told the truth?

Maybe they both did.

One thing was certain: both couples were drinking heavily. Every time I drove out the thirty miles from Austin to visit, I would check the two trash bins alongside each duplex, and both would be stuffed with beer cans. There wasn't a convenience store within ten miles of River Bend on the Colorado River, but they always had plenty of beer on hand.

My stepson Harlan had shown interest in the arts as a young man. While in junior high in 1979, he had borrowed my Super-

Eight Camera and made Monty Python-influenced experimental films, one of them a nightmare vision of a walking water tower monster. These works had gotten him accepted into the Arts Magnet High School in Dallas, where his freshman year he lived in the home of his girlfriend. They had a falling out, however, and he rode the bus down to Austin and moved into the basement of the bookstore with us.

At Austin High Harlan focused on theatre, and one of the plays he had the lead in, a one-act speed adaptation of the long Henry Fielding novel *Tom Jones*, won a first at state. Harlan told me his dream was to be a promoter and not an actor. He paid little attention to his other classes but somehow managed to graduate. Just before the end of his senior year, he jumped up and danced out of a "Just Say No to Drugs" meeting, singing a tune he'd made up about the joys of LSD.

> **He jumped up and danced out of a "Just Say No to Drugs" meeting, singing a tune he'd made up about the joys of LSD.**

He and his older brother Dusty were always into stunts. In 1983 they'd been staying in El Paso with their father and had ordered, delivered right to their door, a large pressurized tank of helium gas. Dentists at the time used helium as an anesthetic. There were no restrictions, and the boys ordered the tank from the same company that supplied dentists and balloon boutiques. They kept the helium in the back of their closet and would get high every day after school, inhaling the gas into their lungs and making the strange but funny helium voices—voices that comics still use today. When his father and stepmother found the tank, they immediately shipped the two boys back to us in Austin. It wasn't until the late nineties that research indicated that speaking games with helium might lead to cancer of the larynx, especially if done in inordinate amounts.

Once out of Austin High, Harlan worked at the bookstore a while, and then moved out to River Bend, where he got a job loading boxes with plastic bags of sprouts for a sprout growing company that supplied grocery stores. His dreams of arts promotion seemed lost in the daily struggle to survive. He'd broken up with his Irish girlfriend, Krista, from high school and later married Cynthia, a woman notoriously promiscuous, who claimed to have been a lover of Willie Nelson. A former biker chick, Cynthia supposedly gave Harlan HIV. This seems entirely possible, because the custom is that biker chicks, on their night of initiation, must have sex with every member of the club.

20

Six months later, at the end of 1993, I was back in Austin from Japan for the Christmas holidays and learned that Sebastian had been in and out of two treatment programs, one run by the city, the other operated by the state. I visited one treatment center at the end of a cul de sac in a South Austin suburban neighborhood, and the counselor told me that he had hopes for Sebastian but that Sebastian had one or two relapses left in him.

> **Each of the stories I heard that night seemed to be full of yearning for the old days when they were drunks.**

I went with Sebastian to an AA meeting off Ben White in South Austin. I had been to AA meetings with my sister a couple of times in Boston. One of the Kennedys was reputed to come to the same group. I don't quite get AA meetings. Sebastian's met in a circle of folding chairs in a nondescript square room with a hard linoleum floor and white walls with no pictures.

Everyone sat down in a folding chair in the circle, and apparently the person who has been sober the longest takes charge of the meeting. Each person takes a turn telling stories of what they were like when they were drunks, how they crashed a car, ruined a marriage, got fired from a job, or embarrassed their children at a school event. Sebastian passed and did not tell a story. I passed too because I did not consider myself an alcoholic, although I could see the group, most of them, didn't take me at my word.

Each of the stories I heard that night seemed to be full of yearning for the old days when they were drunks. Those were the exciting days, the adventurous days. You could hear the tears in their voices for the good old wild days when they did outlandish, dangerous, stupid, and sometimes cruel things.

And each person fed off the story of the others. I felt they were now getting drunk on stories, that they were addicted to stories. To a writer it seemed wonderful. I made mental notes. Some of the stories I heard were worth stealing. Maybe what they were doing was substituting an addiction for stories for an addiction to alcohol or drugs.

> **She was drunk right at the AA meeting.**

But then something happened. A wealthy woman got up to speak, and although she had the line down that these were things she did before she took control and got sober, we could tell she was lying. She was slurring her words. She was drunk right at the AA meeting. I wondered if the facilitator might toss her out on her ass onto the asphalt parking lot, but they let her speak, and eventually she sat down.

Afterwards, they held a little awards ceremony for those who had been sober a month or longer. They passed out chips to these people. The wealthy woman had slipped out. How do I know she was wealthy? By the expensive clothes, shoes, and jewelry she wore.

I disliked the woman. Poor people like my son Sebastian, under great work and survival stress, I could forgive for being alcoholics. I couldn't forgive rich bastards, nor can I forgive most artists, who I believe have a noble calling, essential to society, and have given themselves in service to their particular muses.

I've remained, if anything, a judgmental Protestant, a Methodist from my father's side, although the main reason he made me go to church was that his boss was getting on his case for raising his children wrong. Without strong values, I would not have survived the hippie sixties, being as liberal as I am.

21

The other time I went with Sebastian to AA, during the same trip back from Japan, was on a cold and windy New Year's Eve. For alcoholics, New Year's Eve is the horrid holy night of great temptation, when the hairy beast of drunkenness and addiction stalks the night earth, ready to grab and bite through the clean hearts of any former booze or drug users, who, we remember, never stop being addicts.

So what they do is hold a counter dry celebration, an AA-style New Year's Eve party. Sebastian took me to this set of conjoined steel warehouse buildings off Airport Boulevard north and Forty-first Street. He wanted to go, he said, because it was a great time to dance and pick up chicks. The girls would either be young alcoholics or the children of alcoholics. Once we got inside, that is exactly what he did—go up to a young woman and ask her to dance. He abandoned me to my own devices.

> It seemed this nostalgic band of former drinkers needed this New Year's party as much as the audience.

In one room a rock band played classic country rock songs. Each band member, dressed in long hair and a cowboy hat, testified at the microphone to being an alcoholic and told the audience how long he'd been sober. I felt back in the early 1970s when the cosmic cowboys and redneck rock reigned as ultra cool in Austin. It seemed this nostalgic band of former drinkers needed this New Year's party as much as the audience.

In the next room an old-fashioned country and western band was playing from a low stage. They also did testifying at the microphones. This was so strangely amazing! I never guessed that an AA meeting could be so bizarrely fun. I nevertheless felt lonely, and I wanted to hang a sign around my neck, like you might yearn to do at a gay bar. At the gay club the sign would read, "I am heterosexual." While here, I wanted a sign that said, "I'm a drinker. At times I drink too much, but I'm not an alcoholic."

I continued to explore the place, and eventually found a quiet inner sanctum where the intellectual alcoholics of Austin had gathered. Many of them had beards; many of them were smoking pipes. It's a fact that alcoholics need to find mouth substitutes, some other kind of pacifier, like sipping on coffee constantly or sucking on unlit cigars.

> You get hopeful that your drug-troubled child is going to pull through and come clean, but then, again and again, your hopes are dashed.

I guess I had found my space at the party, but, sadly, in my space there were no women to delight the eye and heart. Not much conversation was going on, either. Intellectuals are not good at small talk. Most were focused on games of chess. I watched the games for a while and sniffed the rich pipe tobacco smoke—in my thirties I had smoked a pipe—but, not having anyone to talk to, no partner, I left and walked back to the first room looking for Sebastian. I was a bit miffed. I'd come to this event to spend time with my son before returning for six more months in Japan, but he was behaving like a teenager who does not wish to be around "old" dad. Deep inside, my emotions raged around. You get hopeful that your drug-troubled child is going to pull through and come clean, but then, again and again, your hopes are dashed.

Had Sebastian gone off with some pick-up to get high?

Ah, the parent gets used to the brush-off. I never located Sebastian that night and after midnight drove back by myself to my good poet friend Melvin Kenne's apartment where I was staying while in the states. Melvin was about to take a job at a Turkish university in Istanbul.

I do not know how my son got himself home from the AA New Year's party that night. We never discussed it. Maybe the young woman he picked up had a car.

21

I can understand why a person becomes an alcoholic. I had a neighbor, Sam, where I live now in College Station, who had a long-term, serious drinking problem. Like Sebastian once did, he worked a stressful job as a short order cook, but, where Sebastian escaped that hard labor, my neighbor cooked most of his adult life for low non-union Texas wages. The heat and stress of a restaurant job could get to anyone. Drug use among kitchen workers is high. Kindly, his parents had bought Sam and his wife an attractive tan brick ranch home across Tree House Drive from our home. He never would have been able to buy a house on the unfair wages he was paid.

Sam and I didn't exchange many words. I never invited him over to my place. What did we talk about the brief times we spoke? The weather mostly, and how the grass was doing in our yards— safe topics. I remember one time he tried to talk Aggie football, and I had to confess I was too cheap to go to the A&M games and had never liked watching football on TV because my dad always got drunk and mean during the games. I wouldn't have mentioned my dad's drinking if I had known then Sam had a drinking problem. I did also point out that I had many friends with serious back problems from playing high school football.

Then Sam's wife, Carol, left him. At first I didn't know why, but when a neighbor told me of Sam's drinking and midnight rages, I thought, can anyone blame her? Alcoholics do tend, over time, to be difficult to live with and to grow more and more depressed because alcohol is a depressant. Not long after Carol left,

Sam shot and killed himself. Because he was my neighbor of many years, I felt a small part of me had been taken. I felt guilty for failing to recognize his signs of trouble. But what good could I have done?

My father had been an alcoholic, and I'd been unable to get him to stop his drinking or his rages. I had made many efforts late in high school and in college. I went to Northwestern University in Evanston not only to save my dad money—he got a tuition break because he worked at a Northwestern hospital—but also to keep an eye on his drinking.

> **Liquor takes many people to a different, happier place for a long time, a place where they feel relaxed and clever.**

Depression and rages—they're part of the problem of alcoholism. Still, I understand why people become drunks. I came close to alcoholism in my own life while living in Koriyama, Japan. I had to struggle mightily to give up my nightly two sake glasses during the year I was home alone every night taking care of my baby daughter Ariel. My wife Sayuri was working nights, and it was nearly impossible, with a child but without a car, to get together with friends who lived in different parts of Koriyama.

Liquor takes many people to a different, happier place for a long time, a place where they feel relaxed and clever. It opens up emotions and people touch base with positive, confidant feelings they may not have felt in a long time. They become better conversationalists and less shy around others. Liquor—at least for the first years—creates a kind of interior utopia, a perfect land of the emotional soul, a watery heaven.

But after time, alcoholics grow depressed and often mean. Their conversation—well, it becomes boorish, repetitive, and all about them because, after all, to many alcoholics, they are the most interesting and clever people on the planet.

22

The odd thing was, although my son was an alcoholic like both his grandfathers, I'd never seen him drunk. Not once. That's how far apart we were—how much he feared me or disliked me and did not wish to share his life. He had seen me drunk, but I'd not seen the drunk in him.

One time, in 1983, when he was in middle school, he had been living in Forth Worth with his mother, Eileen, while she worked on a Physician's Assistant degree. He was acting strange up there, distant, and my former and I both decided it might benefit him if he came and spent the summer with me in Austin. We were no longer living in the basement of our used bookstore and, in fact, had a lovely brick and stone house close to MoPac in the upscale Tarrytown neighborhood.

He had gotten caught and sent to juvenile detention at nine years old.

I made him go fishing once a week with me down on the Colorado River close under the Mo-Pac Bridge, about four blocks from where we were living. He hated fishing, and we never caught a single sunfish or carp although we could see them in the river. I suppose what Sebastian liked best was hanging around with Courtney's children—Harlan, Dusty, and Faith—and smoking pot with them. He must have been just out of the sixth grade at that time.

One Saturday night, after a poetry reading at the bookstore, when everyone had left and we were cleaning up, Sebastian came in the store with Harlan and Dusty. I thought he looked disheveled and strung-out. It had been building up over the months: my worries about Sebastian's distance, his affecting a lost and empty stance around me, and suddenly something inside me snapped. I grabbed his arm and slapped him across the face a couple of times, shouting "Where are you, boy? Where are you? Somebody must be inside. Speak to me!"

Thankfully, my friend, the poet Ricardo Sanchez, came over to where we were standing inside the store's main entry. Gently, he put his hand on my arm. He said what I was attempting to do would alienate my son further. Ricardo, when he wanted to, had a fine talent for diplomacy. I mumbled an excuse, the very kind some alcoholics use, that I had drunk perhaps four beers during the two hours of the poetry reading

"You know," Ricardo whispered to me later, "I caught your boy with a couple of his friends climbing in a window a week ago, breaking into the store after hours, looking for something to steal." At the time Ricardo was down on his luck and living in the bookstore basement where we had lived the year before. "Maybe they were after records or thought they could take the cash box, but whatever, you've got a real problem there with that boy."

I told Ricardo that a couple of years ago, he and some neighborhood friends had broken into houses on the block where his mother lived. He had gotten caught and sent to juvenile detention at nine years old.

Maybe Sebastian was pathological. Maybe something was missing in his brain, and he had no sense of right and wrong. I had read of fathers who, in their elder years, had to hire security guards to protect themselves from their own sons.

> "I caught your boy with a couple of his friends climbing in a window a week ago, breaking into the store after hours, looking for something to steal."

Was that going to be my future? Those fathers I knew were corporation presidents. I doubted I would be able to afford to hire protection.

I'm not big on asking for favors in prayers, but I prayed for the most hopeful, practical favor I could imagine: that Sebastian grow spiritually taller, if not physically taller, than I.

23

There's a speech near the end of Arthur Miller's domestic tragedy, *Death of a Salesman*. Willy has already killed himself using, if I remember right, a rubber hose hooked up to the gas line on the basement water heater. His neighbor Charley, with whom Willy used to play cards, delivers a short speech about Willy, defending his dignity and choices.

"Nobody dast blame the man," Charley repeats in the slang of his era. Charley also remarks that his own relative success in life, with children graduating from college, came about because he was a person who never cared much about anything.

Long ago, in my late teens, when I first read Miller's play and knew it was the first book of my own, about my people—I took Charley's line as a touchstone. Never care too much. Caring gets you ripped up emotionally. I learned the lesson young, when I'd walk the late night streets of Evanston by the city golf course with my drunk

> **You may call this lack of caring a long time coming to love.**

father, listening to his angry ramblings and his promises to stop drinking. I learned not to care when my mother did her suicide attempts as pleas for attention.

Why should I get too tied up emotionally with a mother who said she never wanted to have children and told me to go to a college a hundred miles from home so I could not come home on weekends?

I ignored my mother's requests that I move far away from home for college. My first year at Northwestern University I ran across, in some outside reading in the college library's reserve room, a text of the Buddha's counsel not to desire too much, not to get too attached to the things of this world. I was immediately drawn to this non-Western spiritual teaching. I'd lost my faith in orthodox Christianity years earlier when my father told me the beagle we loved, who had been run over on the highway, would not make it to heaven. "Bugle Anne does not have a soul," my father said.

You may call this lack of caring a long time coming to love. Learning to love may take a lifetime, and I am wary of love. Love is dangerous. Love can get you killed.

24

In 1980 I took both my sons, when they were nine and eleven, to Beaumont, Texas, for three months. Beaumont is in the southeast corner of the state, close to the Louisiana border. I'd gotten a job as a poet in the schools, sponsored by the NEA and the Texas Commission on the Arts. The boys got to come because their mother needed a break and wished them out of the house for a while to see if it would help in finding another mate.

> We drove around the better neighborhoods on trash day and picked up furniture.

We drove down to Beaumont in a camper truck that my second wife, Courtney, generously lent me. I had little money, so I rented a place in a low-rent area that happened to be an Afro-American neighborhood. Train tracks ran down the middle of the street in front of our old ramshackle wooden house. We drove around the better neighborhoods on trash day and picked up furniture. One thing we found and grew excited about, I recall, was a dilapidated pool table with pool sticks and billiard balls.

We all slept in the large front room on sleeping bags with rubber mats underneath, with the pool table in the middle of the room. I got the water turned on in the house but lacked funds to turn on and pay deposits for the electricity and gas. We took cold baths, and I did our cooking in the camper truck parked in the driveway, where there was a propane stove, a sink, and a small refrigerator.

After a few weeks at a local Beaumont elementary school a block away, Sebastian told me he couldn't handle the teasing and playground battles, so I enrolled him in a home school program run out of the state of New Mexico. In 1980, when home schooling was getting underway, the programs were mostly promoted and run by various alternative types, including hippies. The first home schooling convention was held at Greenbrier Commune, close to Bastrop, Texas. Today, home schooling seems to be dominated, in Texas at least, by Evangelical Christians.

Sebastian was supposed to work on his schoolwork in the camper truck while I went in the various elementary schools and taught poetry. Over and over, as the days went by, I would check his work at lunch and around 3:40 PM when school ended. Perhaps I could offer help in understanding some of the subjects he was studying. I don't know what he was doing to fill his time in the camper, but it wasn't much schoolwork.

That's when my "not caring" kicked in. Why should I get all hot and bothered and ruin my day if he was going to be lazy? It was his life, and if he wanted to mess it up, well, that was his choice. What could I do about it? Forcing someone to learn, I decided, is like forcing someone to eat. It's morally wrong and nearly impossible.

25

I n 2006 I called my oldest son Parker on my cell phone. While we talked, he indicated he wanted me to write something for the program of an upcoming tribute concert on Simon and Garfunkel he was doing with his band. The lead line that popped into my head about the 1960s group was that their harmonies sounded generally sorrowful. One of their early hits took the Edwin Arlington Robinson poem about the wealthy Richard Cory who goes home and puts a bullet through his head. Simon and Garfunkel also sang of Mrs. Robinson, a middle-aged woman who is

> **I thought he might know the key to his younger brother's soul.**

trapped in a loveless marriage. They sang about laying yourself down to be a bridge over troubled waters, coming to the aid of a friend.

The two artists came out of the folk movement, a time of surprising hope and promise snuffed out by assassinations. I often think of myself as belonging to the assassination generation. Martin Luther King, John and Robert Kennedy, Malcolm X, and others were all gunned down while we were young and they were in their young adulthoods. In 1968—the same year Robert Kennedy and King were assassinated—the Republican candidate Richard Nixon got elected president by a narrow margin and didn't keep his promises about ending the Vietnam War or about much of anything. For us, it was hard to believe in much, hard to care. So I was part of a numb, often politically inactive assassination generation.

The reason I'd called my elder son in 2006, the reason I called my musician son in Austin, was that he was smart and sensitive, and I thought he might know the key to his younger brother's soul. Parker had never gotten hooked on drugs or alcohol, and he was successful in the music business, so I thought, on impulse the night I called him, that he might have some insight that I had missed, something he might put into words.

Parker, down in Beaumont when we lived in a tough neighborhood while I taught poetry in the local elementary schools, had handled the rough schools well, and later he took guitar lessons.

When I abandoned the family when Parker was six and Sebastian was four, Parker promised Sebastian that he would take care of his younger brother. And yet it's clear they have not remained close. They rarely talk to one another. Parker, for a while, wouldn't let Sebastian in the house for fear he'd steal his musical equipment to pawn it for money to buy drugs.

> **A key is a literary device. It's used in novels or movies when you must simplify.**

Still, being brothers, I figured Parker might know the key, might be able to explain what inside Sebastian's soul made him act the way he did.

Language is an amazingly sophisticated tool, but, at times, language fails. That's why the other languages, like computer code and mathematics, were invented. They have more precision. Perhaps psychology, based in language, fails, and we won't ever have accurate ways of understanding human personality that can point and say, this is what went wrong with the soul's mechanism.

That day when I did get around to asking Parker the "key" question, after we discussed Simon and Garfunkel, I feared he might think I was writing a novel that caused me to do field research by asking such a question.

> **Maybe I could invent a new, genre-busting, literary form—the novel-memoir.**

So I did it in such a way that Parker wouldn't get the idea I was writing about his brother. I came to the subject generally, in a roundabout manner.

"I don't know, man," Parker said. "I don't know if people have single keys that unlock the secret mechanism of how they function. People are too complicated."

"I guess you're right," I said. "A key is a literary device. It's used in novels or movies when you must simplify to give the audience something uncomplicated to take home."

Suddenly, I felt glad I was not writing a novel, and it came to me that maybe I could invent a new, genre-busting, literary form—the novel-memoir. Perhaps such a genre would allow me to use language in a way that it would succeed—or at least not fail so much—in discovering the key to Sebastian's soul.

One thing that was in that moment quite clear to me: one boy makes it as a musician; the other boy ends up in jail, and yet both went through the same traumas.

26

I dated a woman briefly after my second divorce in 1990. We met at the Texas Capitol building in Austin during a demonstration to prevent the first Iraq War. Jackie had left her husband of ten years, she said, because she had lost too much of herself in him. She had been too busy pleasing him and had forgotten who she was.

> "Why don't you quit beating yourself up?"

Well, whose fault is that? I was tempted to ask. She was a tall, boney woman with freckles and a big mop of brown hair. Jackie didn't spend a lot of time gussying herself up in the morning, and I liked that. I knew the relationship was temporary, that she would be headed west to California in a month. I expected at some point she'd tell me she was losing herself, her identity, already, in our short time together, but it quickly became clear she was not.

Jackie loved to hike with those big long loping legs of hers. She had money left from the divorce settlement, her half from the sale of their home. She had no idea what she was going to do with her life yet, but she never got mournful and never said one bad word about her former husband. I admired her discretion.

We'd be hiking up the Barton Creek Green Belt enjoying the mild October weather. We'd stop at times to make love in the woods away from the creek or swim nude in a pool of cool water near Twin Falls. I remembered making love with my second wife, Courtney, along this same creek. I talked to Jackie, as we walked along the trail with the magnificent limestone reaching up on both sides, about my second son, Sebastian, and the pain I felt at failing him.

My new friend was a calm woman but finally got irritated. "You're as bad as the men I've dated who go on and on about their ex-wives. The sons of bankers with stable families become drug addicts. The sons or daughters of happily married lawyer couples, or insurance agents, or real estate agents, become drug addicts. Why don't you quit beating yourself up?"

And you know, for a while anyway, while we were together and after she left for California, I took Jackie's words to heart and repeated them like a mantra when I started beating myself up.

Yet still the terrible feelings came back. Those out-and-out worst feelings, what no father or son should have to go through.

Jackie had no children.

What did she know or understand?

27

Sebastian was disappearing from his mother's house. The year was 1984, and he was thirteen, supposedly in the seventh grade but no longer attending class much. I keep coming back to around this time, as if the key lies somewhere around this time. These disappearances happened sometime before he moved into the closet apartment near the university at sixteen, perhaps to do drugs exclusively.

Sebastian was always so polite. He almost never got angry or used swear words.

The thing is, Sebastian was always so polite. He almost never got angry or used swear words. This cool exterior, this passivity and calmness, was a great front or mask to maintain a secret identity and life.

But he was disappearing. My former wife Eileen and I spent many late afternoons and evenings driving around the central area of Austin, up and down alleys and back streets, looking for our boy. Martin, Eileen's lover at the time, actually tackled Sebastian once as he raced to escape through the long and narrow Adam's Park near Trudy's Restaurant on 30th street.

I talked to many street people all around central Austin, asking them if they knew where my son was. Usually they said, "No," but once I got an oblique hint. Over the years we'd run the bookstore, my second wife, Courtney, and I had helped a number of street people. We'd let them store their gear in our old, broken down camper truck that I'd used in Beaumont. We'd let the homeless we knew sweep the sidewalks outside the store and wash windows for money if they promised not to buy beer. To one fellow with a drinking problem, we loaned two hundred dollars. He said he needed the money to help win his girlfriend back. A former carpenter, he gladly put down his tools as collateral for the loan.

Shorty, black-bearded Shorty, was about five feet tall and had a clubfoot that gave him a limp; he was the one who gave us the hint about our lost son. Sometimes fraternities would hire Shorty to play the clown or court jester and dance at their parties. He didn't mind; his skin was tough from twenty years of ridicule, but he had a good heart, and he knew we were suffering.

"You know about that punk fraternity on West Street?" he asked.

"You mean that big old wooden house that's kind of a parody place, where they've got the day-glow pink Greek letters made of Styrofoam on the side of the building?"

"That's the one."

"Thanks, Shorty," I said. "You need anything to eat?"

"Nah, I'm fine. This fundamentalist minister came through your back parking lot ten minutes ago. He gave us submarine sandwiches for listening to a short sermon."

28

So we drove over to the punk fraternity house in my former wife's blue Pinto, a car I had picked out without consulting her—before we divorced—a car that she hated.

Eileen decided to wait in the Pinto in order to keep an eye on the back door. I went up a short flight of wooden stairs and knocked on a front door that was mostly small glass windows with a sheer white curtain covering inside that I could see partially through. I could tell by the way the door moved when I knocked that it was unlocked, and I was willing to barge in if no one came the door.

But I had never been a drug abuser, and Sebastian knew it.

But a clean-shaven, shorthaired young man came quickly down a staircase to the door from the second floor. I stepped inside and told the young man I suspected my son was in the building, and if he didn't tell me where my son was, he could be charged with a felony for harboring or kidnapping a minor. I would immediately call the police (I was making it all up as I went along.) The young man mumbled quietly—I couldn't hear what—and gestured by nodding his head toward a set of doors, also made of glass, leading to a kind of sunroom.

How often I've written about this event, trying to come to terms with it!

I opened the two doors and scanned the room. Empty bookshelves lined the walls and a cherry wood dining table sat in the middle. No one seemed to be in the room. I looked back at the young man who still stood in the vestibule nodding silently in this direction. I noticed a blanket on top of a built in storage and sitting unit below a bank of front windows. Nothing seemed unusual, and I almost turned and left, but on instinct I went over and pulled back the blanket. There was Sebastian, wearing his usual blue beret on the side of his head and his puffy but dirty silver coat.

The oddness of the situation struck me. Here was I, the longhaired, long-bearded hippie, the radical co-operator of a used bookstore and small literary press, and a low-rung teacher at the University of Texas, about to bust my own son. But I had never been a drug abuser, and Sebastian knew it. I'd never done, at that time, the widely popular psychoactive drug LSD, and, because of asthmatic reactions, I could not bear marijuana.

(A few years later, I would take half a tab of LSD in the front yard outside the main house at the Dobie-Paisano Ranch, and have a revelation sitting under the brilliant stars that, when I shared it earnestly with friends, brought them all to laughter.)

29

Sebastian, for the first time I'd seen, looked drunk or on something—I had no idea what. I suppose the reason why former addicts work in drug treatment programs is because they can tell not only when people are under the influence of drugs but also what they are on. Former addicts have no illusions. They've

> **He slowly reached in his front right jeans pocket and pulled out a white-handled pocketknife.**

been there themselves and know how addicts, out of necessity, shamelessly steal and lie. The famous author and sometime heroin addict William Burroughs called this demand "the algebra of need."

Sebastian then did something that's forever burned in my heart and mind. He slowly reached in his front right jeans pocket and pulled out a white-handled pocketknife. While I said, "You're not going to stab your own father with a knife, are you?" he slowly, almost theatrically, undid the blade and pointed it at me. I could have easily knocked the knife from his hands before he opened the blade, but I wanted to see if he was up to trying to kill or wound his own father.

What happened next remains fixed in the mind's eye in slow motion. No son of mine was going to try to kill me with a pocketknife. I quickly grabbed him by the feet—out of reach of the knife—and pulled him off the bench he was lying on so that his butt hit the wood floor about eighteen inches down. Now that I think about it as I write, I suppose some risk was involved. What if the arm with the knife had somehow gotten behind him, and he had landed on the floor stabbing himself in the back?

Such an action seems unlikely. His arm, when I pulled him off the bench, would fly out from his side instinctively, for his hand to cushion the blow when his rear hit the floor, and that's what happened—yet somehow he managed to hang on to the knife.

No son of mine was going to kill me, no drug-taking thirteen-year-old that was running away and skipping school was going to put down his Ph.D. poet dad.

I had too many books to write and too much life to live.

While he was wiggling around on the floor, he did stab me in the leg through my jeans. That hurt, and I could feel blood running down my leg, but I could sense it wasn't a deep cut. Before Sebastian could swing a second time, I stomped down hard on his forearm and held his hand still. I was wearing cowboy boots so I am sure he felt the pain.

Before he could wiggle free, miraculously, my former wife Eileen burst into the room. Perhaps I had been shouting out her name. She grabbed his arm and leaned on it with all her weight. To get the knife out of his hand, I had to peel off one finger at a time. The young man who had nodded toward the door was gone. We never saw him again. Once I had Sebastian's knife, the fight went out of him, and he became passive. We had no trouble walking him to the car and putting him in the backseat of the two-door Pinto.

We had our boy back. We had him inside the car, but what were we going to do with him?

Both Eileen and I were shaking. We had our boy back. We had him inside the car, but what were we going to do with him? In a flash, in a desperate need for help, I suggested we take Sebastian to Shoal Creek Psychiatric Hospital to check him in. Eileen had once worked at this small hospital, and one of her former lovers, Mack, was night supervisor and could advance him to the front of the list to get him admitted. Such a step seemed better than taking him to court and trying to get him convicted and sent to the juvenile detention center, where he'd been before amongst kids who were drug dealers and murderers. I didn't want to charge my own son with attempted murder.

I wasn't sure, what with my arms and legs shaking, if I'd be able to make the drive safely. Fortunately, the hospital was less than two miles away.

30

As we drove him to Austin's Shoal Creek Hospital on 38½ Street, the thought kept turning in my head: could I ever again have good relations with a boy who tried to stab his father with a knife?

And after that, did I want good relations?

For Sebastian's part, did he want anything to do with a father who smashed his arm so hard, or earlier had slapped his face? I always say, "reality gets bent" during intense human conflict. Different people have different interpretations of what happened, even people not personally involved in the events.

> I have never, before or since, felt so terrible for one of my children, or felt such a failure as a human being.

Oh, the pain of taking your child to a psychiatric hospital and filling out the papers to commit him. Oh, the doubts. I can't describe it. I have never, before or since, felt so terrible for one of my children, or felt such a failure as a human being. I was taking away his humanity, his freedom.

And yet the line from Miller's *Death of a Salesman* about not caring—that came to mind. He was a child, yes, but, through his own childish ways of mistaken thinking, he had created his own destiny. Perhaps I should have left him at the Punk Fraternity House, given him that freedom so he could see where it led? Perhaps I should have cared even less? Oh, but I could not face the

85

thought of his dying there of an overdose or dying in some back alley.

Sebastian had no politics. He was no street poet like the black Beat writer Bob Kaufman, reciting his poems on corners or in bars, making a radical critique of the world. Would he ever be the rebellious artist I had dreamed my children to be? Would he read the gospel of John or the gospel of Henry Miller? Would he be changed, seeing for the first time the paintings of Jackson Pollock?

> **He was a boy who loved listening to the rock band KISS while doing drugs.**

No way. He was a boy who loved listening to the rock band KISS while doing drugs.

Eileen wanted me to contribute to his care on the psych unit. Apparently her insurance was not covering all the costs, but at that time my job at UT was half time for six thousand a year, and the enrollment period for adding people and changing the coverage on my insurance plan had passed.

Courtney and I and her kids were all sleeping in the basement of the used bookstore. Films were made and plays were performed in that basement, art shows blessed the upstairs walls, and poetry readings, along with songwriters' circles, filled the rooms of books with people who sometimes spilled out the large front doors onto the raised sidewalk outside. I was living THE LIFE now with Courtney, the free Bohemian life that I'd dreamed about living with Eileen in San Francisco until she secretly stopped taking her birth control pills. I didn't know how to get back to the straight world to earn good money. I was a down and out poet with no car, no phone, no retirement, and no health insurance, not even a television.

31

The longer Sebastian stayed in the psychiatric hospital, however, the more ridiculous the whole situation began to seem. Four months passed. On every visit he seemed a normal thirteen-year-old kid. Of course, what I did not realize was how enormously talented and convincing Sebastian could be at playing the good boy and how much of his life he kept secret.

I, too, as an older boy, had disliked my parents and all their rules. I resented cleaning my room when told and resented mowing the lawn and having to paint the entire house every third summer. All through high school I had a paper route, mowed lawns in the summer, worked at my father's hospital all day Saturday, and cleaned an insurance office half a Sunday. The hostility to parental authority that built up inside took decades to clear my system.

> My sister and I listened many evenings to our parents fight loudly late into the night, and we cringed in our respective beds.

I had a mother who was housebound, a shut in. I had a father who drank heavily. My sister and I listened many evenings to our parents fight loudly late into the night, and we cringed in our respective beds. I would think about running away; I would want to run away. My parents grew up during the Depression and were unaffectionate. They always pointed out what we children did wrong, and they rarely gave praise—until our later years in high school when Dr. Spock's manual for child rearing became popular.

Yes, I would speculate about running away as I lay in bed listening to rock-and-roll playing on the transistor radio stuck under my pillow, yet, unlike Sebastian, I never did run away. In my mind I never could put together a workable scenario. This was the era of the automobile, and I couldn't drive. How could I get far away and hide? The police would pick me up and take me home. There were child labor laws. How would I make a living? I couldn't feed myself by collecting returnable bottles on vacant lots. Where would I sleep? In those vacant city lots or in city parks? In fields out behind chicken coops where, like a fox in the night, I might pilfer a few eggs?

No, I would need to stick it out, go to college first, and then I could get myself free. College seemed a long way off, but society, I could tell, had things rigged and had you trapped. From another perspective, one might say positively that our society provided young people with goals and direction.

32

Since we lived in Austin, Sebastian could make calculations in the 1980s that I was not able to make in the 1950s. In my hometown of Elmhurst, Illinois—twenty miles from the loop of downtown Chicago—there were no street people and few poor people. The poor you saw were Spanish-speaking Mexicans living in shacks along the railroad tracks working for the Great Northern or the Union Pacific.

Austin was full of street people. My hometown, Elmhurst, had few apartments and mostly middle class homes. Austin was full of apartments, student co-ops, abandoned homes in certain areas, and even an abandoned apartment complex owned by a large corporation out of state, an apartment building that still had its utilities on and where many squatted. Perhaps Sebastian believed he could deal drugs to make a living? Who knows? My intuition was that he did not have a

> **When I came for visits, Sebastian claimed that the therapy sessions were driving him nuts.**

practical mind at thirteen. He did not think these things out. Back then, in the 1980s, no one knew what the new brain research has recently taught us—that the judgment part of the human brain does not fully develop until age twenty-five.

One afternoon, while visiting Sebastian at Shoal Creek Hospital, I told him we were going to make a break from the place. The back stairwell door was unlocked, and we walked five flights down bare concrete stairs, through numerous fire doors, beyond red painted pipes with levers to operate the hospital sprinkler system in case of fire, to the ground floor.

I expected to find there another fire door with the cross bar that sets off an alarm as the door opens, but, no, the metal door was solidly locked. Freedom lay inches away, yet I had failed. Sebastian and I had to climb back upstairs to his psychiatric unit on the fifth floor, back to the sofas, and the TV, and the ping-pong table, back to the group sessions he hated.

"What do I have in common with some forty-year-old housewife who tried suicide because she found out her husband had a mistress?" he'd say.

"Well, you've both gotten off on wrong paths," I'd lamely counter.

Eileen was furious when she learned that someone had tried to spring Sebastian but believed that Courtney had been the one to attempt it. Sebastian claimed, when I came for visits, that the therapy sessions were driving him nuts. He told me they were wasteful of his time and his mother's money. What he needed to do was to get out and return to school, seriously this time.

How foolish we were to take him at his word!

33

I know, and find it sadly fascinating, that you can live with someone a long time, sleep in the same bed perhaps, and yet at the end of, say, twenty-five years, know very little about that person. Of course there are the externals. One gets to know the externals: what people like for breakfast, what their favorite colors are, and whether they like dogs or cats. But of the soul inside, their deep interiors, one may end up knowing little. People don't share everything because they want to keep a piece of themselves for themselves. They know, also, that when they do share, they risk getting belittled or attacked, even by those who love them.

> I had refused to believe any child of mine could want to be anything other than an artist.

Why is that? We ask so many questions when we first meet someone. Where were you born? How about school? What do you do for a living? Then, gradually, we grow incurious. The questions stop. The honeymoon of getting to know one another is over at a time when we might probe deeper and longer, and perhaps be more delighted, if we approached the process of knowing with the long term, curious kind of mind.

But the truth is, most of us don't approach the slow process with such a mind. What we are seeking in the other is not the other, but a person who lives up to our visions of what we want. We stop questioning because we have our own interests and ways of being and don't want the others we depend on to work differently. We don't want to run up against incompatibilities. We actually don't want an *other*; we want our delusions, so we close our eyes and minds.

My first wife, Eileen, either did not believe or refused to hear how strongly I did not want children. Also, she believed in her heart of hearts, that this was not a decision to be shared. This decision was a woman's prerogative. Men went out and got the bacon; women stayed at home, took the paycheck, cooked the meals, and ran the family. Well, she got her desserts, did she not, for her willful blindness, for her not listening?

And I? I had refused to believe any child of mine could want to be anything other than an artist. KISS—grown men prancing on stage in Halloween costumes, playing guitar badly, sticking their tongues out—what they did was so artificially manufactured to please adolescents, was so much about making money by appealing to the cheapest human instincts.

Gene Simmons, I've heard you on PBS radio insulting Terry Gross on her program *Fresh Air*. You're still a jerk, Mr. Former English Teacher, but hey, who cares? You're famous and have made a garbage heap of money. You're retired. Even taking off your white faces could not revive your band's empty and soulless musical career, clown has-beens.

But so what? The nuclear arms industry makes a lot of money. The tobacco industry makes a lot of money. Money, we all know, is this country's sacred cow and its own justification.

Yet Sebastian loved that idiotic band called KISS. In 1985 he came over to the apartment I was living in with Courtney on Manor road in order to stay with me for a while and give his mother relief from the struggle of raising two adolescent boys. We wanted to see if I, the father, could exert a strong influence. At the apartment was a rock band, and Sebastian became its base guitarist. That's the instrument that seems to take the least skill to play. Sebastian, at fourteen, had next to no musical training, but I was pleased to see him taking up something. I believed he needed to develop a passionate interest in something besides drugs. A passionate interest could be his salvation.

Built in the early 1960s, New Manor is a fortress-like structure on a hill. The building is made up of two connected squares that run around the outside of the property. The middle of each square has a courtyard. One contained a swimming pool and hot tub, the other a gardening area and a volleyball court.

New Manor was, in the 1980s, a clothing-optional apartment complex; it was its own little Austin world with locked gates that sealed out the outside world. People went naked in the courtyards all the time. One might think that nudism would be a sexual turn on, but the truth is nakedness quickly becomes prosaic. Some of the New Manorites had utopian faith in nudism and saw nudism as a way to free up the body and bring about some egalitarianism in society since, while naked, you cannot use clothes to declare social status.

I didn't have any real problems with Sebastian while he lived with me at New Manor, and that was because I rarely saw him. After the first couple of days, he stopped coming to our apartment for meals, and then, a few days later, he stopped sleeping in the bed we'd set up for him. When I got home from teaching at UT, I would walk around the complex looking for my boy, knocking on the doors of people I knew, but never could find him. He was around somewhere, but to my eyes he'd disappeared. I imagined that he stayed up all night partying and slept all day. One friend told me he was staying with a woman in her early thirties as a kind of kept sexual paramour.

That day after work I got a call from his mother that he was back living with her.

Since I could not find him, I did the only thing I could think of doing. I went to the manager's office and told them he was no longer living with me and should be evicted from the property. I figured that if no one saw him during the day, one of the security guards was bound, eventually, to spot him at night, and, sure enough, after about a week they spotted him, kicked him out, and changed the combination locks on the doors so he could not get back in. The New Manorites were a bit put out that they had to learn a new combination, but most sympathized with my situation and did not want the apartment to get into trouble for harboring a runaway.

That day after work I got a call from his mother that he was back living with her. Her suburban house was just two miles away. "What happened?" she asked. "When I talked to Sebastian, he seemed to like living with you there."

"Sure he liked the place," I said. "What fourteen year old boy would mind all the sex he ever dreamed of with an older woman? I couldn't do much with him because he never came to our apartment, and I never saw him," I explained.

"He said you kicked him out for no reason."

"Oh, he knows the reasons," I replied. "He never heard me speak them because I never saw him."

For a short while I'd found one thin straw to grasp onto that came

> **Would Sebastian find a calling in music as did his brother —or at least a way to earn a living?**

from my son's stay at New Manor Apartments. Although I barely saw the boy, I'd heard occasional rumors that he'd been practicing hard with a rock-and-roll band. Sebastian seemed to be taking an interest in an activity beyond drugs, beyond hanging out with drug buddies. His brother Parker was passionately involved in classical music and never had to be told to practice his viola.

Would Sebastian find a calling in music as did his brother—or at least a way to earn a living? Perhaps he also had musical talent.

Another reason I saw his interest in music as a straw to grasp onto was his older stepbrother, Dusty, also played rock-and-roll. His band rehearsed in the basement of Books Plus. So far his group had found just a few shows to play at a small bar off Congress even though the keyboardist didn't seem to have her scales fully mastered, and none of group could sing well. But Parker was superb on the electrical guitar.

One problem was the cocaine. The drug is a way to overcome stage fright, and cocaine lifts the ego and convinces its users their wildest dreams are possible, that their talents are unlimited. I recall Parker telling me at the bookstore counter that it was just a matter of months before they'd do a spot on the Johnny Carson show.

My eldest son was playing in the high school orchestra. Sebastian, a drop out, was playing in a heavy metal band at the

Manor nudist apartments. That's why I knew my hopes were a thin straw. The rock-and-roll scene in the 1980s in Austin was awash in drugs, and being in music could make life worse for Sebastian, as it had for Dusty, who eventually went to prison for stealing his other band member's equipment to maintain his cocaine habit. Music is often promoted as good for brain development. The research is there, and it can do that. The dangers of the culture of music—especially rock and popular music—might, however, be overlooked by parents.

The practice room was actually in a crawl space under the house.

One good thing did happen: after Sebastian was ejected from New Manor Apartments, the band began holding practice in his mom's house where she could keep an eye on him. I helped get the space ready. The practice room was actually in a crawl space under the house, so we had to dig the dirt out and carry it into the backyard as well as move objects deeper into the far corners of the crawl space or put them somewhere else in the house. I remember digging up rusty wrenches and trowels flung into the crawl space by previous house owners. I was always nervous in that house—not because of my former wife or her long time lover—but because when they had first moved in, everyone had gotten lice, and the lice had transferred to me and to my current spouse, Courtney, and her three children.

We spent days boiling clothes and rubbing the poison shampoo product Rid into our scalps, then scrubbing and washing it out. What finally worked for me was an herbal remedy purchased at Whole Foods Grocery Store, Rosemary Shampoo. Fortunately our grubbing around in the crawlspace to make a practice room did not result in another infestation of lice.

It took a week to get the crawl space cleared enough so that the teenage boys could actually stand up and practice. All the music equipment—amplifiers, microphone stands with mics, drums, power cords, special effects pedals—got moved in. They each had a place to stand in front of a microphone to play and sing. The heads of all these tall, thin, pale boys must have been about a half inch below the rafters.

Putting them in the crawl space was a brilliant idea. The sound of heavy metal was muffled more than if my former Eileen had given them a basement room or a bedroom upstairs. Moreover, with access to the practice room our boy had less reason for running away and disappearing.

Still, people in the house had to suffer through these four boys sawing and banging away on their instruments, trying to imitate KISS and other bands. The noise remained horrendously loud, like a scalpel scraping over slate right beside your ears, and Eileen was lucky none of the neighbors called the police to complain. Heavy metal is bad enough, but adolescent boys learning to play heavy metal, well, I have to give Eileen credit. That's about like placing yourself in some lower level of hell. She did it for love, to give Sebastian an outlet for his energies and to keep an eye on him.

I could stand at the entrance to the crawl space and listen for fewer than ten minutes. I can't say I ever heard Sebastian's baseline amongst all the noise. He was learning on the spot as he tried to scream/sing and play along.

He told me shortly after giving the band up about two years later that he'd never seen it as a career. They got a good deal of practicing in, and they actually improved, but they didn't get to the point of playing in any clubs.

> "You're fine," she told me. "You're not crazy."

The week before Sebastian moved back to his mother's and I was desperate to find out where he was hiding in New Manor, I walked with Courtney to Books Plus.

Once we opened the business I found I couldn't sit still, so I paced around the bookstore, from History at one end to Romances at the other. But I still could not calm down.

Finally I told Courtney I thought I was cracking up and needed to go to the emergency room at Brackenridge Hospital, though I wasn't sure what was bothering me. All I understood was that I was jumpy and couldn't sit still or concentrate.

As I walked through a park near the hospital, I started weeping. Somehow the tears clarified what bothered me. It was Sebastian. I tried without success to put the boy out of my mind.

"I'm here to check myself in," I told the lady at the front

window of the emergency room. "I'm going crazy."

Instead of filling out stacks of papers, the clerk summoned a social worker, a woman wearing a full-length white coat. She led me into a quieter part of the hospital to some comfortable chairs, and she asked what troubled me. Her eyes were kind.

"My son," I said. "I'm so worried about my son." Tears flowed again.

The social worker sat with me while I wept. When the crying stopped, I felt much better.

"You're fine," she told me. "You're not crazy."

When I left, it felt as if heavy sandbags had been lifted from my shoulders, for a while, anyway.

34

Maybe I'm the one to blame for Sebastian's difficulties in school. The business with the alternative school down in Beaumont in 1980, when I forgot and didn't finish the paperwork by sending in a final report that was required—well, that set him back, and then I did another thing, another small thing I suppose. This was in 1984, before he pulled the knife on me. This was early on, when he first started ditching school.

I took him across the street from the new Rio Grande location of our bookstore, to Conan's Pizza, on a hot September Saturday afternoon. The bikers who owned the place named it after the sword and sorcery fantasy character Conan the Barbarian, created by West Texas author Robert Howard, who'd committed suicide shortly after his mother died. The meek mama's boy Howard had created a commercially successful alter ego in the heroic, muscular barbarian Conan. The bikers and their crew always made a tasty pizza in that dark but small restaurant that is today still in business. After we finished our meal—Courtney and Eileen were there too—I tried to show Sebastian by doing a little math on the back of a Conan's place mat why it would be impossible for him to make it on his own.

If he made $3.50 an hour, the government would take fifty cents of that for taxes and social security. That would leave him with three dollars an hour. He'd take home $120 a week or $480 a month. A tiny single

Why go to school when he'd have one eighty a month for spending money?

room, if he could find one in expensive Austin, would cost him two hundred a month. That would leave $280 for groceries and entertainment. If he cooked over a hotplate in his room and did not eat out, groceries would take about $25 a week. That would leave him with $180 for everything else.

My son Sebastian looked at me and stared into my eyes. He'd never had one hundred eighty dollars in his life.

"You won't be able to buy a car or pay for gas on one eighty a month," I told him.

He didn't care. Most places he wanted to be, he could walk. Free UT shuttle buses ran through the interesting central part of Austin where he wanted to live. The drivers never checked to see if you were a student when you climbed on board.

Yes, the boy had stars in his eyes. Why go to school when he'd have one eighty a month spending money?

"That's forty-five a week," I said. "How are you going to afford clothes?"

The boy wasn't listening. Sebastian was blinded, dollar stars in his eyes.

35

The year is 1995, and I'm back for good from Japan after four years out of the United States, with a new wife and a new child. My new, third wife I'll call Sayuri, and my three-year-old daughter I'll call Ariel. Sayuri was a successful businesswoman in Japan with her own English language school, translation service, and advertising agency. We got to know each other when I hired her to translate some of my poetry and fiction into Japanese.

Our daughter Ariel is for me, among so many other things, an atonement child. I hope to get right with the cosmos by raising this girl in the best way possible. Slowly I have been trying to let go of parts of myself, some of the Bohemian parts, and trying to act more middle class. It is not an easy transition—I'm not sure I can pull it off—but Ariel is a child that Sayuri and I consciously decided and worked to have, and, although I am forty-six and she is thirty-nine, we took the calculated risk we would remain reasonably healthy into our sixties to raise a child. I was allowed to assist with the delivery by the Japanese woman doctor on November 13th, 1991.

> **Slowly I have been trying to let go of parts of myself, some of the Bohemian parts . . .**

As I look back I wonder if it was truly me who was speaking about a third child. Perhaps what I remember was the strong voice of my second wife, Courtney, who adored children, so it was her voice running in my head. But ultimately it does not matter. When

I'd asked Courtney in 1990 to have a child with me, she said I was "too irresponsible." She preferred an insult to admitting that, at forty-eight, with a grandchild, she might be too old to have a fourth child.

Near the end of 1994, the high-paying university job with Texas A&M in Japan collapses. The city of Koriyama cuts off the school's funding and the campus closes. I recall walking the hallways of our school building, one of the last teachers on campus, seeing paper posters by creditors attached to computers and desks claiming the equipment for money owed. Yet kindly, the A&M English department back in Texas offers me a low-rank position, even though I have not asked for one. With savings from Japan, we are able to buy a pleasant three-bedroom house about fifteen minutes by car from campus, depending on the traffic.

We're not back in the United States more than ten months when I get a call from my sister. She's concerned about our mother living alone in San Angelo. It takes seven hours to drive from College Station to San Angelo far out in West Texas. My sister lives in Boston and can't afford often to fly down. Karen is going through a divorce and is having psychological problems. I, too, have been concerned about my mother since the stroke she had in the dentist chair getting her teeth removed.

Mother can no longer speak.

Together, my sister Karen and I come up with a scheme to move my mother to College Station to live on one side of a duplex. While I was in Japan, my sister transferred power of attorney over my mother's finances to herself. We can take a part of my mother's funds to make a down payment on a duplex close to my house.

After thinking and talking it over for a week, my sister, Karen, and I decide to invite my son Sebastian to live in the other side of the duplex. Sebastian has a new partner, Pearl, a girl of eighteen he met in an Austin pool hall, and we have been getting up at seven in the morning on the weekends to drive the 3 ½ hours down to San Antonio to visit them where they live on the western side of the city. Sebastian is working at the Golden Corral Restaurant.

We take a walk along the River Walk and visit the Bracken-ridge Zoo we used to visit when Sebastian was a small child. The stately elephant rides are gone, but the miniature train still clacks and clangs under the tall live oaks and pecans in the park. On another trip we go out to the hill country town of Medina, where Pearl, now Sebastian's common law wife, spent much of her childhood. We have a chicken fried steak lunch with Pearl's grandmother in a local restaurant and then go out to the hill country land where they keep horses.

Pearl is seven months pregnant with her first child, and she puts Ariel, who is now four, on a mare in front of her, and takes the mare jumping. She does not bother to ask either Sayuri or me if this is all right. I am worried about Pearl and about Pearl's baby. What if all the jumping motion of the horse sends Pearl into labor? We are a good distance from a hospital. I am worried, too, for my own daughter. What if Ariel falls off the horse onto the hard, hill country, limestone ground?

Am I older and perhaps more conservative than when I tried to get Sebastian onto the elephant at the San Antonio Brackenridge Zoo? No, I'm not. I'd never put someone else's child on an elephant, on a horse, or in a hot air balloon, without first getting a parent's permission.

36

I remember Sayuri and I making a later trip to San Antonio, this time to look for Sebastian. He'd disappeared, and Pearl had returned to Medina to stay with her grandmother. Somewhere, he must be off doing drugs. I rang the doorbell of his apartment, and, when no one answered, I peered in the window. All his belongings and furniture were there, but after several random checks back to look inside during the day and at night to make sure Sebastian wasn't hiding behind the sofa or in a closet, I was fairly convinced the boy wasn't living in the place. The manager of the complex, understandably, wouldn't let us into the apartment even though he knew I was Sebastian's father and realized no one seemed to be staying there.

We went to the Golden Corral Restaurant where Sebastian once worked and talked to the manager. Sebastian had told me the manager makes one hundred thousand dollars a year but has to be at the restaurant seventy hours a week.

No, the manager informed us, Sebastian has not been coming to work. The manager said that Sebastian was an excellent worker, and if he showed up again, he would be glad to put him back on the job. We drove back to College Station, north on Interstate 35 and then east on Highway 21, arriving home around ten. I was sick with worry. I didn't know how I to handle the situation. My wife Sayuri was supportive, but when

> **It must be similar to what parents of soldiers in a war zone feel.**

105

your child is out there and you don't know where he is, there's a tenseness that fills your body. It's a tenseness that will wake you in the middle of the night over and over, like when the rent is due the next day and you know you don't have the cash, and, if you get evicted, you don't know where your family will go to stay. It must be similar to what parents of soldiers in a war zone feel. You don't know where your child is, and you don't know for certain if your child's alive

Fortunately, my poet friend Hedwig Gorski sent me an email. Have you lit some candles for your son and said a few prayers? she asked. The tone of her email was, "What are you thinking, poet? Have you no imagination? Have you no sense of magic?"

The truth is I didn't have much sense of magic. I grew up in a house of doctors who believed in science and rarely went to church. Science couldn't cure the pain felt, but the candles did help. I found myself believing, trusting that the votive candles of Jesus and the Virgin of Guadalupe I'd lit and placed around our home would offer protection for Sebastian.

37

Given this disappearance, why then did I go ahead with the plan to allow Sebastian, Pearl, and their new child to live on the other side of my mother's duplex? Sayuri was against the plan from the start. My sister and I, I guess, were acting stupidly, and we didn't know how else we could afford to care for our mother. Pearl told Sebastian it would be a good opportunity for him to get to know his father. Instead of paying rent on the duplex, Sebastian and Pearl were going to provide assistance in caring for my mother.

Pearl and Sebastian were not happy with their situation in Dripping Springs where they got back together following Sebastian's disappearance. They had a child now but both needed to work full time to pay bills, hospital delivery expenses, and childcare costs. Sebastian was twenty-five. He had passed his GED and had been off the street for a couple of years. He had taken training and now worked in a nursing home taking care of the elderly. Pearl was working at a Dairy Queen.

> **Pearl had taped to the refrigerator a piece of paper that read, "I love you, Sebastian."**

I was missing my son and yearned to be near him now that he seemed himself again. My former wife Eileen was not happy with the idea. She did not think her son was ready for such responsibility. I, too, had cold feet and doubts, but my sister Karen was gung ho about helping both Sebastian and our mother.

"It's good for fathers and sons to be together," my sister said. "And it will be great for both of you to be around Mom. She's easier to take since that stroke in a dentist's chair took away her ability to speak."

Sebastian and Pearl pulled into College Station on an early Saturday afternoon on the first of September in 1996.

"I like this town," Pearl remarked. "Not too big, not too small."

Their first child, Gwen, a girl, was asleep in Sebastian's arms when they came in our house. Pearl was pregnant with a second child. Later, when we took them over to the duplex to help them unpack, I noticed Pearl had taped to the refrigerator a piece of paper that read, "I love you, Sebastian." The duplex had a fairly large backyard, and Sebastian fantasized about getting a dog. The house had two bedrooms, a kitchen/dining area, and a large living room.

Located ninety minutes north of Houston, College Station in 1996 was a boomtown containing new retail shops everywhere, large and small, with big signs on their doors begging for help. Sebastian got a job at a fancy nursing home on Rock Prairie, got fired in a week for some reason, and then landed a second nursing home job a few days later. Pearl got hired on at Subway but was fired in two days. They got their young daughter into a Head Start Daycare for free. Pearl landed a job at Wendy's but was fired after a week for arguing with the boss.

I was not happy that Pearl was taking these jobs. She was the one who was supposed to prepare meals for my mother while she cooked meals for her family. She was the person who was supposed to check on my mom now and then during the day and sometimes at night while Sayuri and I were at work or asleep.

Sebastian and Pearl managed to get a credit card and started buying things at the nearby Wal-Mart on FM 2818: a stereo, a kitchen table and chairs, a couple of dressers. I was surprised that they were able to get credit or would want credit. My house was filled with furniture bought at garage sales.

I'd provided my mother with an electronic device with a button that by radio signal rings a bell on Pearl and Sebastian's side of the duplex. It was supposed to be for emergencies, but my mother rang it three and four times a night, and it was Sebastian who kept getting interrupted to go over to take care of grandmother's needs.

"Are you all right?" I asked him. "You look terrible —exhausted."

"I'm all right," he assured me. "Pearl is pregnant. It's hard for her to get up."

I helped late afternoons after classes at A&M and on weekends and checked with them every evening. The story I had been told about my mother by my sister was that Mother was doing exercises, riding a special bicycle even, to get her strength back after her stroke. She was also supposedly working with a speech therapist in San Angelo, but when she got to College Station, she couldn't walk or talk. She had to spell out what she wanted by tapping out letters displayed on a laminated sheet of paper.

Getting mother out of bed and into the bathroom to use the toilet or to take a bath was heavy lifting. I pulled a muscle in my back and for a month slept fitfully with the pain. I went to a chiropractor and started using an exercise machine. The chiropractor did nothing for my problem, but the exercise machine worked wonders.

38

But I was worried about my son. He told me that one night, when Pearl came to pick him up at the Shenandoah Nursing Home where he worked, she got tired of waiting in the car and stormed into the building demanding that he leave.

Sebastian and his wife got into a yelling fight at the nursing station. He kept insisting that he could not leave until all his work was done for his shift.

> **"If he's gone back to drugs, I'm going to leave him," she told me.**

I'd told Sebastian right up front on the phone that he should not come to College Station if he had drug issues. I'd also told him, directly and frankly, that if the drug problems came back, he'd have to leave. Pearl had told him also that she would break up with him if he went back to drugs.

"Don't worry," Sebastian said. "I'm doing fine."

It was great to have my son around. He had developed the ability to talk and was no longer silent. My wife Sayuri said he was the handsomest man she'd ever seen. He was a real sweetheart—humorous, thoughtful, and polite. He and my four-year-old daughter, Ariel, grew close. All six of us went for picnics at College Station Central Park. The kids loved the ducks there and loved playing on the fancy playscape. Sebastian would push Ariel on a swing. I would carry Gwen on my shoulders in spite of the pain remaining in my back.

But then, on a blustery weekend toward the end of November,

Sebastian disappeared. Pearl called me up and was frantic. "If he's gone back to drugs, I'm going to leave him," she told me.

After four long, painful days, Sebastian reappeared.

"I got locked up in jail in Navasota," Sebastian explained.

> **I still lacked a sense of how drug users can lie so brazenly.**

"I went through a stop sign by mistake and they locked me up for outstanding warrants from back in San Antonio."

Since he said it all with such a straight face, nonchalantly looking me in the eye, I wanted to believe him. I still lacked a sense of how drug users can lie so brazenly. I'd been living in Japan away from such dramas.

Later I picked up the phone and called the jail in Navasota. The town has seven thousand people and is twenty-six miles south of College Station on HW 6 toward Houston.

"My son, Sebastian Bern, says he was locked up in your jail for four days. I don't know whether to believe him," I said coolly. "You'd think he would have called to ask me to post bail."

"Hold on a minute," a woman's voice said on the phone. A minute later she was back on the line. "No, we've had no Sebastian Bern housed here."

The next evening I went over to the duplex to see my mother. and I told Sebastian, when we were alone in the front yard, that'd I'd called the Navasota jail, and they had no record of him.

Sebastian didn't bat an eye or pause when he said, "Oh, I gave them a false name. I didn't use my real name."

I knew this was a lie because if he'd used a false name they'd have no outstanding warrants from San Antonio to hold him on, but I didn't call him on the lie.

Maybe I should have.

"What name did you use?"

"I forgot already. Something common like Bill or John."

39

I'd told my son that if he went back on drugs I'd have to kick him out of the duplex. Pearl remembered my words and came to me. "It was a slip up, I know," she said as we sat at her kitchen table. She'd fixed me a cup of instant coffee that I couldn't drink. "I'm going to give him another chance. Can you?"

"Well, I've always tried to practice the Christian notion that justice should be tempered with mercy."

Without saying whether I believed his Navasota alibi, I told Sebastian I would give him another chance. How in the world, in such a short time in conservative College Station (home of the Bush Presidential Library), had he gotten reconnected to the world of drug dealers? Had he been hanging out at a crack house? Sebastian worked full time, had a child, and took care of my mother. How did he find the time to locate a crack house or find dealers to supply him?

I felt bad for Sebastian. This was not turning out to be a good arrangement for him, working in a nursing home forty hours a week on the evening shift, and then having to take care of my mother. Pearl wasn't much help,

> **But then Sebastian disappeared again.**

and I was paying him nothing, just giving them one side of the duplex rent-free. I felt like I was exploiting them both, but I had no money to pay because I was paying a mortgage on my own home and on the duplex. I had childcare costs for Ariel. We couldn't afford to eat out or to take jaunts or weekend getaways. Yes, I felt sorry for Sebastian, sorry for us all in this situation. I tried to help as much as I could by taking care of my mother on the weekends. I would sit at the table in her kitchen and grade papers while she lay in bed and watched television. I kept thinking how the statistics show that caregivers often die before the people they are caring for pass away.

But then Sebastian disappeared again. He was gone for a month. In the second week Pearl went to Austin with her little girl, Gwen, to stay with her mother. I had a key to the apartment but no key to the padlock they'd put on the side gate, and I remember bringing my lawnmower over to the duplex, wrenching my back worse lifting the mower both in and out of the trunk of my small black Isuzu, and then hauling it through their apartment, not worrying about the grass stains or dirt being left behind on the carpet, to get at and mow their backyard.

Pearl returned without Gwen the third week and far into her second pregnancy. Yes, she had talked to Sebastian, and yes, in spite of words to the contrary, she was willing to take him back, willing and waiting—and thinking she was going to continue to live free in the duplex with her family. I'd probably go back on my word and make the same decision if I were an eighteen -year-old woman with no means of support and a small child, and with another on the way.

40

I found a woman to spend the day taking care of my mother. My sister paid the costs from my mother's savings, which she'd transferred to her Boston account. Sayuri, Ariel, and I would visit with Pearl, and all of a sudden she would ask me to drive over to Texas Avenue by myself to the Dairy Queen to buy her a chocolate Sunday. She was expecting a baby and had cravings. Gwen was with the grandmother in Medina.

No matter how many times she asked, I would do it. My Japanese wife, Sayuri, was stupefied.

"Don't worry," I said. "I'm humoring her, letting her think she can boss me around, getting her off guard. Soon the hammer is going to come down. She's beginning to think I'm her puppy dog slave and I'll jump at her every bark, but, as soon as she goes into the hospital to have her baby, I'm changing the locks on the duplex. She's doing nothing for my mother. She's got no lease, and she's not working, so she's out. I can't afford to support her, and we don't know if Sebastian will ever show up again. We'll keep her clothes and stuff in boxes in the garage for her to pick up."

> **Sebastian was gone the next day, back to his secret world of drugs.**

People usually see me as a mellow, easy-going guy and are often surprised and shocked at how coldly I can bring the hammer down. Here I was kicking out my daughter-in-law just after she returned from the hospital from having a baby.

My son, Sebastian, did not show up on the day Daniel was born, but six days later Sebastian and I found ourselves sitting together in his old Buick in front of my house. I was about to show him the way to the hospital on Rock Prairie to visit his wife and new son. My four-year-old daughter, Ariel, was playing in our large front yard. When she spotted Sebastian, this look came over her face that was both happy and sad. She had heard Sayuri and me talking about his use of drugs and his disappearances.

Ariel didn't know whether to come running up to him for a hug or to run away. Sebastian saw her standing there, and I said to him, "She's confused, Sebastian. She doesn't know if you're here to stay or soon to be gone."

"She's confused!" Sebastian shouted in an angry outburst, looking over at me next to him in the Buick, but said no more. Yet there it was, still close to the surface of his soul, still fresh and unhealed, the pain of my abandonment when he was four.

I wanted to say, "That was then; this is now." I wanted to say, "I'm sorry for your pain and for what I did, but you are only allowed to blame your parents for your troubles until you're twenty-five. Then you're on your own—no excuses."

Sebastian was gone the next day, back to his secret world of drugs. When Pearl was discharged from the hospital, my former wife Eileen's husband, Harrel, was there with a U-Haul to take her back to Medina. Sayuri and I drove over to the duplex to see if Pearl had managed to get all her belongings in the U-Haul Harrel had brought.

"Where are those metal shelves?" she said she had noticed them gone from the duplex.

"They didn't belong to you," I said. "They came from our garage. We loaned them to you. The same's true for the washer and drier."

"You'll never get to play with your grandchildren," she said.

"Pearl, stuff it!" Harrel yelled, getting up in her face. Harrel was a master of pretending to lose it. He could turn on and off acting crazy like turning a light switch off and on.

I didn't say anything. I already loved my new young grandchild; I had loved them both from the first moment I held each one, but I didn't say anything. I was a Midwesterner. I was the grandson of a no-dancing, no-drinking, and no-card-playing

Protestant Irishman. We'd been taught to bite our tongues. In Texas I'd learned to be more openly expressive, but it had mostly gotten me into trouble. In Japan, and from my third wife, Sayuri, I learned again to zip the lips, to be more careful in what I said.

I'm friends with Pearl now, and I see my grandchildren by her as often as I can.

41

What is this thing called—not love—but blood? When I was young I was convinced I would love those who were worthy of love and had some form of noble pursuit. My father may have been for many years a drunk, but he'd had a noble pursuit: to cure heart disease through his research on cholesterol. I was not going to care for somebody merely for blood, just because we shared genes.

When I look at my son Sebastian I see little of myself. I see his mother—the same marvelous red-black hair, the same creamy, robust white complexion. His body is not built like mine at all. It does not have the Celtic or Scotch-Irish thinness. He loves to work with machinery, and he loves to cook. I can make spaghetti, burgers, chili, and steak. That's about it, and no matter how hard I try, be it an automobile or a computer, machines do not like me to fool around with them.

For the next eight years I didn't see or hear from Sebastian.

What is this blood? I know my ideas as a young man to live amongst artists in San Francisco are Death Valley dead, as dead as an old cow's skull on a ranch near Big Bend. I can only read and dream about such a life in the serene and Buddhist beat poetry of Joanne Kyger, Gary Snyder's first wife. I never found a large enough supportive community of like-minded artists in Texas to form a community. I tried. I put up signs in the Whole Foods on Greenville in Dallas and at other locations, proposing to turn my Woodedge house an hour from Dallas into an artists' commune. No one replied.

Instead it has turned out to be blood where I have found strong and meaningful connections. Is this the way we have been created by society, or is it in our genes? Is it, as the sociobiologists claim, based on a drive to survive our own mortality by reproducing? I don't know. All I know is that it's there and incredibly powerful, the pull of the community of blood.

For the next eight years I didn't see or hear from Sebastian. He made no effort to contact me and did not write me back or return my phone calls. Much of the time he had no phone. When he did have a phone and answering machine, he would not pick up. Sebastian had a lot of people after him. He left Pearl about ten months after I'd run her out of College Station. I will admit I have a big problem with women who try to order me around, especially if I am not married to them and they are not my boss. I don't think it's a sexist issue. I have the same problem with men.

A few weeks after Pearl left, I was out trimming the bushes at the duplex's back fence, cleaning up to rent out the apartment that Sebastian and Pearl had stayed in. Things were happening fast. My sister had called and said Mother's money was all used up. I had to let the woman go who had been watching Mother. It was one of the hardest things I've ever had to do since I admired Carmen so much. I also needed to move my mother to a nursing home. Medicare was now paying her expenses. The duplex was not a fancy place, but we'd planted some trees outside, painted the doors, and redone the trim around the roof.

I was getting the duplex ready to show to prospective tenants when the gentleman who lived on the other side of the fence started speaking to me through the tall bushes. He was a tall, thin, reticent, and melancholy man. I don't remember his name, just that he seemed so disappointed. His downturned mustache added to his air of melancholy.

I remembered that Sebastian had borrowed my green Chevy van to replace the roof on this fellow's duplex for extra cash, but the man had grown nervous on how long the job was taking. He was afraid the place might get rained on with the shingles off. The ceiling and his stuff inside might get soaked and ruined, so he called a professional roofing contractor. The company gave him almost no discount for the work Sebastian had done and so Sebastian got paid a mere forty dollars for his two days slaving and sweating in the sun.

I got angry with Sebastian because, when he brought my green Chevy van back, it was filthy inside, full of chips of asphalt shingles and the tiny stones from the shingles. I had to rip out the yellow shag carpet on the floor, throw it out and then sweep the van out. Another small thing that would irritate Sayuri and me about Sebastian and Pearl was if they asked for money to buy something for my mother or for the duplex, and I gave them, say, two twenties, they'd never give us back our change or at least show us a receipt, even if we asked.

Sayuri grew more upset about this behavior than I did. In Japan nearly everybody is scrupulously honest. I felt terrible about the way my mother was waking Sebastian up so often at night. I felt he deserved the money although we couldn't afford it. If mother had treated him better and not bothered him to exhaustion, perhaps he would not have gone back to drugs. Ah, but she was lonely and craved attention and affection. Even if all you were doing was carrying her to the bathroom to use the facilities, it made her feel, I think, a little loved.

42

So for eight years after the collapse of the system we had set up to take care of my mother, I did not hear from my son Sebastian. I don't think I've ever experienced anything so devastating. Divorces, true, tear you to pieces. Probably not a day goes by for the next five years that you do not think of your former spouse in either a positive or negative way. But this was blood; this was, strangely, different. The old saying lawyers quote during divorce negotiations is, "Blood is thicker than water," meaning that in the end the children mean more to the parents than the parents do to each other.

> No doubt Sebastian has his own narrative to explain why he broke off contact.

For eight years I lost the desire to write or to publish. For a writer, writing is life. I lost the ability to sleep and had to take various brands of prescription sleeping pills that would work for a while but then would become ineffective. Some nights I would have a reverse reaction to a sleeping pill and become completely manic, racing around the house most of the night. My memory got so foggy in the exhaustion I'm amazed I did not lose my teaching job.

I managed to hang on to my position because I was so low on the status pole and received a low salary. I was not expected to publish. When, as a family, Sayuri, Ariel, and I watched a film or a video or a DVD in which something painful happened to children, I could not stop myself from crying.

No doubt Sebastian has his own narrative to explain why he broke off contact. Perhaps he feels I did not appreciate the killing labor and loss of sleep he put up with in taking care of my mother. Perhaps he wanted revenge, to hurt me back for my abandonment of his childhood. Perhaps he forgot or didn't believe me and take me at my word when I told him I would kick him out if he went back to using drugs. Perhaps he was terribly ashamed at how he had behaved and couldn't believe I would forgive him.

When he disappeared the second time, I wrote a series of angry letters to him at his mother's Austin address. In one letter I asked him, what did he expect to come from a relationship with an underage runaway he'd picked up in an Austin pool hall notorious for drugs, fights, and police busts? In another letter I mentioned that I'd talked to the neighbor behind him, who had said he was convinced Pearl must have fried her brain by doing too much angel dust. Whatever the drug is, the name is ironic. That was why her mind worked so poorly.

So the news that made it our way in bits and pieces all those devastating years I did not see Sebastian was as follows: (1) he had left Pearl; (2) although he was still married to her, he was now living with another woman, Teresa, in south Texas a few miles from the Rio Grande River and the Mexican border, outside Edinburgh; (3) he had gone to trucking school, become a truck driver, and was making the best

> There had never been a clearing of the air. I was afraid of it.

money of his life; (4) unfortunately, he got pulled over in Missouri for speeding and they had him thrown in jail for nonpayment of child support; (5) the place he was living in outside Edinburgh belonged to an uncle of Teresa and was a complete dump; and (6) my former wife Eileen claimed that he did not wish to see me because the place they lived in was so derelict.

I hungered in forlorn hope with every crumb of news about my second son. I missed Sebastian. It felt as if a large hole had been blown through my body.

What a strange, closed-mouth animal I was. How did I get that way? Sebastian acted the same way with me. We never discussed my divorce from his mother. He never heard my point of view. Just thinking of trying to explain tied me in knots. We never discussed why, when in junior high, he skipped out of school and later ran away from home. We never discussed why he'd moved off into a tiny one-room apartment or why he'd pulled the pocketknife on me.

There'd never been a clearing of the air. I was afraid of it. I was afraid he'd start shouting, and I'd start shouting, and worse things would be said that could never be taken back.

43

Maybe what we needed was a therapist. I tried it for one session with Sebastian and my former wife Eileen. We began the sessions before the time Sebastian quit completely going to school, back in 1984 when he was thirteen. We met in a female therapist's office over on the east side of Austin. The room was small, and we all sat up close to the her large black desk. She was younger than Eileen and I by about ten years, and she seemed kind and competent.

The purpose was to discuss Sebastian with the therapist, but somehow Eileen ended up directing the conversation, so we spent the whole time talking about our divorce eight years earlier. Perhaps she felt the need to do this to set context for work on Sebastian. Still, I felt beat up and resolved never to go to therapy again. Today I have no idea what Eileen said about me at that session. Did she make accusations? I've blocked it all from my mind.

> **I had little time to give to Sebastian—not that he wanted time.**

That year I had made another effort to get close to my son. Eileen, who is five feet tall, said she could not always handle Sebastian; at thirteen, with his size, he scared her sometimes. She wondered if I might take him in for a while.

I wanted to try again to reach him. The bookstore had moved from downtown into an old grocery store building on Rio Grande where there was more customer traffic. The rent was much higher but we had better parking. The place downtown had just two parking slots and was dying a slow death from lack of customers and revenue.

The main problem with the new store was the smaller living space. Our needs for space were always changing depending on how many of the second wife's kids were with her and how many with her former husband. At the time, none were staying with the El Paso former husband. Fortunately, the oldest boy, Dusty, was out in San Francisco with his girlfriend Glenda, both working in the porn industry. Faith and Harlan were with us. Our space had no kitchen and no place to take a bath. We had a room for Courtney and myself and a room for Faith. Harlan lived in a kind of closet area behind a set of bookstore shelves.

My plan was to let Sebastian sleep on the sofa of the store after closing at nine. My former wife and I were in the early stages of discussing this possibility when she made the mistake of mentioning it to Courtney. They both got into a huge fight. Courtney had been tense all year. She hated living in the back of the store, especially after the fancy house in Tarrytown, even though she had been the one who refused to consider renewing the lease because of her dislike of the landlord. She wanted me to set her and her kids up in a decent rent house, but I refused to do so because she refused to go out and get a good-paying job as a legal secretary. She believed working for lawyers was a major selling-out of the soul and instead worked part-time in the store and did typing to barely get by.

I was down in my underground windowless bunker of a University of Texas office when I first got a call from Eileen explaining her point of view. I shared the office with a couple of other instructors, and it was embarrassing to be talking about my personal life over the telephone.

As soon as my former wife hung up, the phone rang again, and it was my current wife, as angry as the former, now telling me her side of the story.

"Look," Courtney said, "I've been seriously thinking of moving back to El Paso for good. If you bring Sebastian into the bookstore, I am out of here."

"Hold on a minute, Courtney," I said, even though uncomfortable with my colleagues listening in. "We made a promise to each other to always be there for our kids, to always take them in if they needed help and a place."

"Your former's got a big three-bedroom house. I'm telling you I won't have it."

"What about the time I slept on the living room floor with you so Dusty and his girlfriend would have a place to stay after they couldn't pay their rent?"

"I'm just telling you. I'm about a hair's length from splitting from here and splitting the blanket with you."

And so I backed down. My job was stressful, taking up most of my time and energy preparing for classes and grading papers. I was teaching three classes of advanced composition and one section of American literature survey. I wasn't in a place to handle fights between women, and I had little time to give to Sebastian—not that he wanted time. I spent around twenty hours a week at this punk restaurant that had few customers. The only way you could tell the place was punk was by the clothes the waiters and waitresses wore. One day I heard them discussing how they had never known their grandparents.

I would order a beer or two and eat a hot lunch, and I'd stay in a back room alone grading papers for six or seven hours on the days I wasn't teaching classes. The life of a composition teacher is characterized by long hours devoted to the heavy grind of grading endless piles of papers, and always the pressure of more papers to come. In the last few years, the number of papers assigned has thankfully been decreased for college composition teachers.

44

Courtney ended up leaving Austin in June of 1984, supposedly for good, in spite of the fact Sebastian never moved in. Courtney was disturbed that we were living in the actual year of George Orwell's book, 1984, and feared a totalitarian take-over at any moment along the lines of the book. It did no good for me to remind her that Orwell had merely reversed the numbers for the date of publication, 1948, so the numbers had no special significance.

She sent her daughter to El Paso and told her son Harlan he could have her share of ownership in the bookstore. Her reasons for suddenly abandoning us all were murky. She did not like living in the back of the bookstore on Rio Grande and 29th. The space had no shower and no proper kitchen. When she wasn't working in the store, she was spending her time typing student papers for income, and that left her no time to do her own writing.

I didn't take Courtney's pronouncements about leaving Austin forever seriously. If missing her husband weren't enough to hold her here, missing her sons and daughter, who loved Austin and never planned to leave, would bring her back. I advised Courtney to pick up a class at the El Paso Community College to support herself, and she took my advice for once and got a composition class. I packed most of her possessions into my

> I remember the great German writer Goethe saying of his one son, "He is not one of the Gods."

Plymouth Volari wagon and I drove her out to El Paso where she found a trim white stucco house in the lower valley across from the Tigua Indian Reservation. If the U.S. turned George Orwell 1984 totalitarian, we could swiftly slip over the border of Mexico. I stayed with her through much of the summer, and every night we got to listen to the Tigua Indians drumming in the parking lot of a convenience store right next to our home.

I was receiving unemployment for the summer of 1984. UT never let me know at the end of the spring semester if I would have a job in the fall. To get close to my son, this boy who, not long ago, had tried to stab me with a blade, I made plans for the two of us to travel from El Paso up to the Grand Canyon. I would make a meager amount by selling books from my small press in the bookstores on the way, and Courtney would mail me my unemployment checks to general delivery in various agreed-on cities.

I was nervous about the trip to the Grand Canyon. My father had visited the place in 1964 and told me about how the mules walk along the outside edge of the trail that snakes its way down to the bottom of the canyon. My dad had said the mules were trained and sure-footed, but about every few years one slipped and fell to the bottom with its rider. The night after my father's story, I'd dreamed that if I ever visited the Grand Canyon, I would die.

I'll never forget that first day Sebastian and I spent traveling in my 1976 slant six Volari wagon. Headed north on an Interstate, we'd reached Albuquerque, New Mexico, at about 3:30 in the afternoon. All my thirteen-year-old son could think of was buying clove cigarettes. The high and dry July heat wasn't bad when we were winging along the Interstate with the windows open, but it was not so jolly slowly tooling around Albuquerque in stop-and-go traffic looking for special cigarettes.

I remember the great German writer Goethe saying of his one son, "He is not one of the Gods."

Pretty snobby, I admit. Yet you'd think, after all our years together, my son would have picked up on my way of living as the spiritual calling of the artist. You'd think he might have felt a little of my feelings that making art was about as close to the divine as you can get.

Nope. He wanted cigarettes. We spent the rest of the afternoon finding a head shop that stocked the little square salmon pink boxes of clove cigarettes imported from India, and he immediately began stinking up the car with the cloying smell. I'd bought him six boxes, not knowing if we'd ever find another store that carried the product on our Grand Canyon journey.

Never underestimate the power of words. That is my poet's faith. My grandfather called cigarettes "coffin nails," and his graphic image made me a nonsmoker, unlike the two daughters he raised. I called cigarettes "coffin nails" in front of my sons all the time, but with Sebastian the image didn't stick.

45

I was still relatively young then, just forty-three years old. On a tree-shaded side street south of the University of New Mexico campus, we both slept well in the back of my Volari wagon on a rubber mat I rolled out. The next day I visited two bookstores near the university, plus the campus bookstore, and managed to sell an amazing seventy dollars worth of books. Sebastian remained tolerant as I spent most of that second day going from store to store. I can't remember what he did, except to hang with the freaks at the university's hippie park, smoking more clove cigarettes and perhaps sharing joints.

> **Sebastian wasn't talking, mainly just chain-smoking clove cigarettes.**

The next day the trip took us farther up Interstate 10 to Santa Fe, where we visited the Hall of Governors from when New Mexico was part of Mexico, but I had no luck selling any books at the many stores in that town. We camped in a national park in the mountains above Santa Fe. Paying was on the honor system, and since we were tight on funds, I sacrificed a little honor and didn't pay. It was cold but gorgeous up in the forest. The sharp pine smell was fresh and invigorating.

From there we drove through Los Alamos, famous for the atom bomb, and then on to Farmington in the northeast corner of New Mexico. Sebastian had seemed tense the whole trip. Perhaps his mother had forced him to go. Perhaps he was thinking of when

I had stomped on his arm to get him to let go of the blade. Perhaps he worried this trip was a subterfuge to take him to Cal Farley Boys' Ranch in West Texas outside Amarillo. I'd looked into enrolling him there after he ran away to the punk fraternity house and we first suspected he was heavily using drugs, but the expense, at that time, was well beyond our means. Now the ranch is tuition-free for parents, funded by generous donations.

Since Sebastian wasn't talking, mainly just chain-smoking clove cigarettes, I made a valiant effort as I drove Highway 44 to fill the empty silence. I kept running on and on about how beautiful the desert southwest was, and how I wished there was a way we could all afford to live there. I kept talking about the colors of the clay, the desert sotol and ironwood, the quaking aspens along streams, and the wonderful mountains—things that have little interest for a fifteen-year-old boy. I praised the remoteness, too. There were fewer people in the whole state than in Houston, Texas. I talked about how good it was to be able to see so far without seeing a single human habitation. I told him about the Indian pueblos and that some of them were the oldest continuously occupied cities in the United States.

What was on my mind when I was fifteen? Since I was an odd-ball, I can't use myself as a model of the typical. All I could think of then was young women's bodies and how I wanted to lie close to their warmth and make love to them. I'd heard the teachers in school joking about how all the girl students talked about was boys, but, from what I could gather, they thought of boys mostly in terms of social settings—a cool guy maybe with some status being on an athletic team to take them to a special dance or to a movie.

The girls of my school liked boys for status reasons, especially as related to sports, not for who they were, so, although I dreamed of making love to whichever gal I had a crush on that month, I did not find any of them particularly interesting. I recall almost coming at my desk in freshman English class sitting next to a school cheer-leader. She was so stereotypically blond and Sandra Dee beautiful that I hated myself. In my high school most of the women students planned to get married and have children right out of high school. I had no interest in anything like that. There was way too much life that needed living. This was before Vietnam and before assassinations of leaders and presidents. The whole world seemed to call with its siren song.

Were sexual hormones—fueling images of girls' thighs and breasts—driving my son to smoke clove cigarettes all day? I had no idea. He was not talking much. At least I could be fairly sure he was free of all drugs, except nicotine, on this trip.

I had little money, and he had none.

46

We were on our way to the Grand Canyon, but I kept thinking of the prophetic dream I'd had in college after my father told me of his trip. By making this trip with Sebastian, I hoped I was going to stare down superstitions and fears.

We reached Farmington, a plain-Jane kind of a town, in the early evening. We decided to go to a drive-in movie before finding a side street in which to sleep in the back of the station wagon. I wish I could remember the title of the movie we saw—something like *Dreamweaver*. It was a cowboy and Indian flick, and the only part I remember is the main Indian character fleeing up a mountain and being chased by the other main character, a white man. The white man was an expert tracker, but the Indian kept hoping he would meet up with other Indians from his tribe to help him out. The Indian was unarmed while the white carried a rifle and a six-gun.

> **He belonged to a strange new generation—one I did not understand.**

The Indian would make these bird-like whistle sounds in the woods up on the mountain, and all around us at the drive-in movie, from the other cars, we'd hear the same bird whistle sounds. Sebastian and I quickly understood Indians surrounded us. I tried myself to make the same bird call whistles, but Sebastian signaled me to quiet down. They would know we were not Indians, he said, and they might come after us.

"Okay," I said, "I'll stop, but it sure was fun trying to get the sound right."

An unusual feature of the film is that the lone weaponless Indian won. I don't think anyone got injured or killed. After much suspense the Indian escaped. I liked seeing a movie where Indians won and wondered why more weren't made.

"I identify with Indians; don't you, Sebastian?" I said.

"Not particularly," he said.

"They're outsiders," I said.

He didn't say anything back. I began to think how he was enough of a risk-taker to risk his long-term health and life with drugs, but was too conservative to play around copying Native American imitations of bird songs in a drive-in movie in Farmington. He belonged to a strange new generation—one I did not understand.

47

The next morning we drove to the downtown postoffice to see if Courtney's letter with my unemployment check had arrived by general delivery. Each week I had to fill out a form listing the places that I had applied for jobs. I made these places up. One I recall was "Keats' Kitchen" after the famous poet Keats; the other was called "Samuel Johnson's Pizza" for the great dictionary writer.

We got a nice newsy letter from Courtney down in El Paso, but along with the letter my weekly unemployment form was returned. Even though I had looked over the form carefully, I had forgotten to check one small box. I would need to re-mail the form and wait another week to get the check. This wasn't the first time I'd forgotten to fill out something on a form.

I counted my money. Sebastian and I had enough to live on if we continued to sleep in the station wagon and stick to peanut butter and jelly from a supermarket. I didn't mind it much. It was an adventure, and I had the company of my son. I had plenty of books along to read. At the moment I was in the middle of Tolstoy's *War and Peace*. We could hang out under a tree in some park. It would be an exciting challenge to avoid the police and not get arrested as vagrants. If we did get arrested, well, then we'd have softer beds to sleep in and slightly better meals.

But we did not have enough money to go to the Grand Canyon. When I told Sebastian that, for one of the first times in his life, he became furious. His face got red and he started swinging his arms around. Once before, I could remember him this angry. That'd been four years earlier, in 1980, when he'd been nine and we'd been sleeping on the floor of that derelict house in Beaumont on the street that had train tracks going down the middle. Every night, about four a.m., a train would rumble through about twenty feet from our front door.

When preparing to leave for that poet-teaching job, I'd packed some of my magical equipment from the days I had been a magician in high school. I thought perhaps I might use the equipment in some of the schools I was visiting. I also bought more equipment in Beaumont, and Sebastian successfully put on a magic show for all the kids in the neighborhood. We moved the pool table into the kitchen, and the kids crowded into the living room and sat on the floor to watch Sebastian do his tricks off an old card table.

> "You're coming," I insisted. "I'm not leaving you at home near that pothead guy who lives across the street and is three times your age."

Then it was his older brother's time to shine. Parker had been taking guitar lessons. I'd offered them to Sebastian too, but he'd not been interested. Parker was going to have a recital at the music store downtown by the library where he met his teacher for lessons.

Sebastian got furious. "You're not dragging me to some boring recital where kids play the same stupid tunes on their guitars one after another," he growled.

"You're coming," I insisted. "I'm not leaving you at home near that pothead guy who lives across the street and is three times your age. Plus, Parker came to your magic show. You need to be a decent brother and come to his event."

It had taken Sebastian days to get over his anger at that one. Why didn't he want to go hear his brother play the guitar? Was it the usual sibling rivalry, or was that hippie guy across the street, the only other white person in the neighborhood, turning Sebastian on to marijuana or something stronger?

The thing is, I never, never, not even once, saw Sebastian take any addictive drug except coffee and cigarettes. The one time I ever saw him high was when he pulled the knife on me. This son of mine, his mind worked so differently from mine, and he was so good at keeping secrets. Up in Farmington I think we finally gave up waiting for my unemployment check, and my former wife Eileen wired us money.

48

Since we were running out of time and had given up going to the Grand Canyon we started back, traveling east on Highway 64—a bit out of our way—to visit the town of Taos, made famous by D.H. Lawrence; it's now an arts community located near stunning desert close to the Sangre de Cristo range of mountains. The famous actor and movie director Dennis Hopper had lived in Taos in the 1960s. I stopped off at two bookstores in Taos. In the first store I bought a hardback on sale of Susan Sontag's *Under the Sign of Saturn* and asked the owner behind the counter if she'd be interested in purchasing or

I knew Sebastian was angry with me for my poverty and for my flakiness and failure to take him to the Grand Canyon.

putting on consignment some of my publishing company's books. She took a quick look at what I had and said no.

The second store in Taos was a long narrow place run by a burly Texan. I put on his counter about five paperbacks I wanted to buy and then asked him if I could leave some titles from my company on consignment. Consignment meant he did not have to pay up front. The store would only need to pay if, when I wrote an inquiry, titles had sold.

The Texan said that he'd learned over time that consignment books never sold, and so he'd stopped taking them.

"Well, I guess I'll pass on these," I said.

I was the only person in the store. It was hard to imagine how Taos, a small town then with a fine library, could support two bookstores. The Texan looked startled. Perhaps he'd lost his one sale for the day.

Sebastian had come in the bookstore with me. When he got back on the street by my Volari wagon he said what might be the one kind and supportive thing he ever said to me when he was a child, "Sorry you're having so much trouble selling your books, Dad."

"Nobody reads anymore," I said bitterly, "but this is supposed to be an arts community, and you'd think I'd find a bit of support here."

I knew Sebastian was angry with me for my poverty and for my flakiness and failure to take him to the Grand Canyon. He had a good reason to be angry, and I appreciated his surprising words of kindness. I was actually relieved not to be going to the Grand Canyon. I still have not visited that magnificent hole carved by the Colorado River—and probably never will. Dreams have always given me wise counsel. I take seriously mine about the mule, with me on its back, falling off a narrow trail to the far bottom of the canyon.

It was also a dream that told me to divorce my second wife Courtney.

Sebastian and I arrived back in the lower valley of El Paso late the next day, and the next morning I drove to the El Paso Airport, surprisingly close to the Franklin Mountains, and I put him on an indirect flight through Dallas first and then on to his mother in Austin.

49

Is the distance between my son and me a repetition of the distance between my father and me? My father was an easygoing and trusting man. He would allow me, on Saturday nights after I got my driver's license, to be gone with the family car until 2:00 a.m., but he never would have allowed me to smoke clove cigarettes—or any kind of cigarettes. My father's main interests were getting drunk, usually on beer, watching sports on TV, and doing cholesterol research at the hospital where he was chief pathologist. He had two research labs and two lab assistants.

> Is the distance between my son and me a repetition of the distance between my father and me?

I take some interest in cholesterol but next to none in sports. My father bragged he had never read a book since graduating from college, and I read two or three books at the same time, all the time. My father was often drunk and angry at the dinner table, upset with those who had more power than he at work. The whole family kept quiet to avoid his outbursts. I grew up relatively unambitious because my father was heavily competitive and ambitious, and his drinking turned him unhappy and mean. Perhaps too much of my lackadaisical personality has rubbed off on my second son. He is not afraid to work hard but doesn't seem to have much ambition for advancement. Perhaps, like millions of Americans, he feels trapped by the need to work constantly and sees no way to advance.

Why did I allow my son to smoke those awful cigarettes? Because I wanted no more fights. He had tried to stab me with a knife. I did not want to unleash that hostility again. I wanted him to love me at least half as much as I loved him. I know my father was disappointed because he never felt I cared for him as much as he believed he cared for me.

I can recall the exact moment in 2004 when I saw my son again after eight years. His two children from his second marriage often spent the weekends in Austin with my former wife Eileen while their mother, Pearl, worked, caretaking at nursing homes. I would often take them to a small park around the block. The kids liked throwing a tennis ball into a small creek in the park and seeing my golden retriever, Biscuit, leap down the ravine into the creek water and fetch the ball.

Sebastian was driving a truck full of cantaloupes from Edinburgh to Dallas, and his plan was to stop and see his children. He parked his truck along Airport Boulevard and then walked to the park after picking up his mother, Eileen, at her nearby house. We gave each other a long hug right in the street next to the park.

"What's it been, eight years?" I said.

"Something like that," he said.

50

I began to sleep better after our meeting. My memory improved with the better sleep, and a lot of the physical aches and pains I had and attributed to old age began to lessen. Since that time, I've spoken to Sebastian often on the telephone and even made a number of six-hour drives down to South Texas to visit my son and his family now that he's living in a less dilapidated place.

His wife, Teresa, has been welcoming of my family in her large mobile home and even took us for a ride to South Padre Island. I was amazed that she had six relatives living on the same street as Sebastian and she lived on. Cousins and brothers were always dropping by, and I would take whole gangs of kids Teresa was related to, along with the eldest grandchild Alvco, hiking along the irrigation canal next to an orange orchard close to their doublewide.

> **Sebastian and I never discussed his disappearance from the duplex.**

Sebastian and I never discussed his disappearance from the duplex when he was living in College Station and helping to care for my mother. Not for one moment have we ever danced close to the topic, although Sebastian does know that my mother passed away from heart failure in 2002.

Sebastian did tell me the story of going out to the country to see my former second wife, Courtney, and her children. One trip, he said, was enough. Sebastian as a child had been close to his step-sister Faith. She was two years older, a smart and beautiful blonde, and I think Sebastian had always been impossibly in love with her.

"Dusty wouldn't come out of his trailer," Sebastian said. Dusty is the eldest stepson and must be fifty now. He is still spinning records in a tittie bar and was still doing, Sebastian believed, a lot of alcohol and cocaine. The police had been out to the property many times, and Dusty had grown paranoid. His wife had left him, come back, and then left again. He had raised one son by a previous marriage, Dusty Junior, but that boy was now in prison.

Poor Dusty. His childhood dreams had turned to dust. He was born dyslexic with a wandering eye, so he could never do well with studies in school. Yet he loved to play the electric guitar, and after quitting high school, he tried hard to make it with a rock-and-roll band made up of friends from near Dallas, but then one member was killed in an automobile wreck on the way home from practice. We moved to Austin in 1980, where he made new friends and formed a new band called Life's No Paradise. I felt the band's name reflected the disillusionment of these children of the counter-culture.

It was his new Austin musician friends that got Dusty into cocaine, and they must have grown to regret it because he started hocking the band's musical equipment to maintain his habit. That was easy to do because the band's practice room was in the basement of our bookstore. His best friend, Calvert, took him to court, proved his case of theft, and Dusty went off for a few months' stay in the county jail, choosing to serve out his sentence rather than deal with the complications of the Texas parole system.

Their band, not surprisingly, was dead, and his friends went into the t-shirt business. When he got out, Dusty met a beautiful, black haired woman while subbing for another musician at a fraternity party, and she was as slant-eyed as he was. She'd just flunked out of UT, and her father, a corporate executive, was trying to set his daughter up for experimental brain surgery he hoped would rewire her brain to function normally. Dusty and Kate fled first to Oakland and then to San Francisco. The only work they could find was in the porn industry. His girlfriend got into speed, and Dusty did more cocaine. Eventually he hocked his guitar for drugs and gave up on his music dreams.

"Harlan's still the alcoholic," Sebastian continued, bringing me out of my thoughts about Dusty and back to the present. "Being HIV positive doesn't seem to have done him much damage, I guess, 'cause he takes his medicines. Still, he's pretty skinny. I bet he spends more of his S.S.I. checks on booze than on food."

51

My former second spouse, Courtney, had finally given up on Austin as too expensive and bought ten acres in the country thirty miles east and south, not far from Smithville. At first she had lived on the land in a small tent. Now the members of her family each own their own trailers.

"Courtney's boyfriend, Farmer, was swaying around drunk, too," Sebastian said. "I talked to him about truck driving, and he was interested in becoming one. I didn't explain that he'd have to pass a drug test."

Sebastian went on. "I don't know what I saw in that way of life. I don't know why I thought those people were so cool. Courtney was the most sober one, but, of course, she was always stoked on marijuana. I was glad to get out of there. I don't plan on going back."

Sebastian's stories made me angry all over again at my second spouse, made me believe that it was her influence and the influence of her children that set Sebastian off on the wrong path. When Courtney and I first got together, she was coming out of a religious phase and wouldn't even drink a glass of wine. When she told me two years later in 1977 that she was going to go back to smoking marijuana, as she had done before joining a fundamentalist church, I did not raise objections. Marijuana was cool then, and everyone smoked some, it seemed, except me. We were in Salt Lake City then, happily crowded into a small apartment where she seemed to be doing well in the Ph.D. program in creative writing, and I was enjoying being CETA poet-in-residence for Salt Lake

City. Little did I know that, in a year, she would suddenly decide to leave Salt Lake City and then, shortly after returning to Texas, she'd one day throw her reading list across the bedroom and announce she was abandoning her Ph.D. studies although nearly completed. Did the marijuana impede her judgment--produce in her a delusional optimism?

I often felt so.

How much of the hard times my former spouse Courtney eventually went through can be blamed on drugs? I don't know. All I know is that Courtney spent a period of time homeless in Austin until, with some financial assistance from her mother, she moved to the land in the country near Smithville. That was years ago, and her boyfriend Farmer has now passed. Before he died, Courtney herself had a stroke, but over the years she has been slowly regaining her ability to write and speak and has done readings and published work.

> **I've wondered if he feels more forgiving, having himself abandoned his own two kids . . .**

I feel Courtney remains a heroic woman, one who has gone through impossible times but always remained a survivor. Her hard times may be less due to her marijuana smoking than to her dedication to hippie and Bohemian values, her radical opposition—though she is in no sense a Marxist—to patriarchal society and capitalist labor, and to her unlucky choice in husbands. After her experience with her first husband and with me, Courtney gave up on marriage and lived with Farmer, with whom she felt she had achieved her most successful heterosexual love relationship.

She deeply grieved his passing.

I've often wondered if Sebastian feels more forgiving toward me now that he has been married three times, as I have been married three times. I've wondered if he feels more forgiving, having himself abandoned his own two kids at ages younger than I abandoned him and his older brother.

I've been tempted to ask but haven't. We don't discuss intimate topics. I don't know why. Is it a male thing? Sebastian is certainly smart enough, and I do discuss such topics with his older brother Parker.

52

Acouple of times Sebastian has abandoned his truck and disappeared for a few days. He's never paid back his mother the large tuition she paid for him to go to Ralph's Trucking School north of Waco. At one point he got into a big disagreement with his third wife, Teresa, and they split up, and he went back to his second wife, Pearl. She went with him on a truck run, but the romance of the road quickly wore off, and they split.

Pearl remains the wild child whose judgment does seem impaired by Angel Dust done at a young age, as the neighbor claimed. She's thirty-one now. For a while she was taking Gwen and Daniel into convenience stores and teaching them how to shoplift. She's worked in such stores and knows the tricks.

So Sebastian and I talk on the telephone every couple of weeks, especially when he's driving one of his big rigs across country. It's amazing. He might carry a truckload of fruit from one coast to another searching for a buyer, or at least he used to. That may have changed since the gas prices shot up. He seems to have the major roads of the entire country memorized and to know his way around nearly every American city with over 100,000 people.

He tells me he likes the solitude of truck driving. He seems to gain solace and strength from the mere movement of the truck itself, and he must be off drugs or he'd get caught in the drug tests they give truckers. He drives long hours, and he sleeps little—that's how you make money when you are being paid by the mile. They do have new laws that are supposed to protect truckers' health and get them rested so they don't fall asleep at the wheel and run over cars and people, but these laws only slowly seem to be changing truckers' behaviors. I still find myself behind swerving, late-night truck drivers.

Sebastian is always tired. He is always way behind on sleep.

I couldn't lead the life he leads—being on the road six days a week and home only one day. He works so hard because he's inside a machine, inside a small but rigid economy, that demands hard work. He has substantial child support payments to make to his second wife. He now lives in his third wife's grandmother's house in a city that's as south as the tip of Florida. Unemployment is high, and Mexicans from across the border keep the wages down. They've got few trees on the property and run their air conditioner day and night most of the year. He has big electric bills to pay and pays high tuition for his two children to attend a private Christian school.

Sebastian bitches over the phone when he is driving. He complains that his wife hardly works and won't clean or do laundry, that all she does is lie around the house reading romance novels. He complains that she spends all his money and has no concept of saving. He complains that she has a car and he does not.

"But you drive a truck," I say, "and you're in that truck driving out of state most of the time."

"I'm thirty-eight years old, and I should have a car, given all the money I make and pay out," he says.

Sebastian earns a higher salary than I do. Both my sons earn more money. You don't become a poet/college teacher to grow wealthy. Sayuri and I get by with tight controls on our spending and by living in a town, College Station, where expenses remain relatively low.

My dear readers, in the rest of this book, I will continue to grow more philosophical and do less story telling. The philosophy I believe necessary. It is my attempt to ride down deeper in the submarine of words, to explain in ways useful to others with drug-troubled children what were the causes of my son Sebastian's drug problems and how he eventually recovered.

I hope you stay with me through the rest of the book and gain some insights useful to your struggles. I will understand, however, if you drop out at this point, having finished the basic story.

Whatever you decide to do, thanks for being here!

53

I look at both my sons, and I don't understand either of them. Does a father ever understand his sons? Both men are divorced and are required to make large child support payments. Both seem to me womb slaves, trapped by women into living lives they don't want to live to bring in large amounts of cash. I could never live the way they live. I'd flee the country and go underground, run off to Japan to teach ESL, or go to Korea or the Middle East.

And yet, I think my boys are content. At times my elder son Parker is on the verge of having his electricity turned off. Sebastian now and then will miss a child support payment, but Parker has become locally famous as a musician, and he's doing exactly what he loves, playing music. He's not getting to play his first love, jazz, and he's not getting to write songs and lyrics, but that may come in the future. He and his new main squeeze are both musicians, both Bohemian, and they seem to have a good time together, living together in far south Austin on an acre of land with a large garden, great friends, a dog and cat, and numerous humorous ducks and chickens.

Bashō, the Japanese poet, wrote that the man who did not love children would no longer be able to see the beauty of flowers.

Sebastian—he has his solitude behind the big wheel of his truck. He needs his time away from people, much like my mother needed time away. Sebastian loves his kids, and he loves his wife, and his work has purpose and meaning because he is doing it for his family. That's the way blood works. Maybe that's the way of the human universe.

I still don't understand Sebastian. In his thirties and a father of four, he continues to do stupid things. A few years ago he bought a trampoline and leaped off the roof of his mobile home onto the trampoline. The canvass of the trampoline hit the hard ground before it tossed him up in the air and into the prickly Saint Augustine grass. He wrenched his back and is still recovering. His first child, Erica, from his second marriage, broke her arm on the trampoline by flipping off onto hard packed ground full of nasty stickers. She now swims for her high school varsity team and is building confidence and having a blast. A tall girl built for athletics, she's gained strength and slimmed down but broke her arm a third time roller-skating. Amazingly, they've been letting her swim with a cast on.

My other son Parker—the musician—has not filed an income tax return in years. He knows one of these days "the revenue men" will come for him. Being self-employed, he has rarely paid much into the social security system.

Womb slaves—both divorced, both paying high child support? I am not against children. Bashō, the Japanese poet, wrote that the man who did not love children would no longer be able to see the beauty of flowers.

54

Y ou know, I need to stop being so rough on my sons. I need to stop being the wise ass, acting as if I possessed some kind of advanced, divine wisdom. These men are not womb slaves. This is a kind of novel-memoir and that means the author must beware getting trapped within his own limiting memories. All my life a blind and bizarre idealism has worn me out and misled me, sending me down wrong paths and making my judgments of others too severe. Womb slave is a literary term I like to throw around, developed from reading the Beat writers, especially Mr. *On the Road*, Jack Kerouac. My two grown boys, in spite of their occasional complaints, are happy, and that is the best of blessings.

If we didn't have children, we'd hang out mostly with people like ourselves. How boring! Children and grandchildren force us to stretch, to learn new things and be more than we have been.

Do I understand anything? Is there a key? I grew up in a family that moved around. In my childhood I lived in Duluth, Saint Paul, Minneapolis, San Antonio, Seguin, Elmhurst, Chapel Hill, and Evanston. Looking back at my family's transience, I can see some negatives, although when we were growing up my parents always spoke of the moves in positive terms. Dad got a raise, and we got to see different parts of the country and see how different kinds of people lived.

Moving can make you adaptable and open-minded. My own children and stepchildren lived in El Paso, Salt Lake City, Edge-wood, Beaumont, Arlington, and Austin. My belief about moving around tends to remain positive, as my parents taught, but my stepdaughter Faith has told me that moving so frequently interfered with her and her brothers' abilities to form lasting friendships and feel connected to a community. New to a city, they usually ended up hanging out with the troubled lonely outcasts who tended to use and abuse various drugs.

I almost replied to Faith, coming as I do from what I call the assassination generation, "Why would anyone want to feel connected to a community? Don't you want to feel above, a part of a greater international community of artists, like the writer Faulkner or the painter Cezánne?"

Faith, my dear Faith, for a while, worked as a housepainter with her boyfriend, got addicted to speed, and dropped to ninety pounds. But before that, in 1986-87, she truly did desire to become a musician. She tried to learn to play the saxophone, pretty much on her own, but her saxophones kept disappearing from her room, probably stolen by her older brother, Dusty, who had a cocaine habit to support and stole valuable items out of the bookstore and out of our household drawers. In 1988 he rifled through his

> **People tell me the older I get, the more I'm like my father when he was this age.**

younger brother's superb private record collection to steal the rare and valuable discs for quick resale at the trendy used record stores of Austin.

I remember my wife Courtney crying the second time Faith's saxophone disappeared. My first wife, Eileen, had to pay off a note, since she had kindly cosigned on the loan for the second instrument. We had no money to pay for the stolen instrument. Faith, who had such a good, quick mind, dropped out of high school at sixteen like her oldest brother, Dusty, and moved out of our apartment with a friend of hers from high school whose mother was a trucker heroin addict. The friend and Faith had a short lesbian affair.

After dropping out, Faith worked as a flower saleswoman on Austin's downtown party zone, Sixth Street, and then, when she turned eighteen, managed a bar. How old, legally, do you need to be to manage a bar? Older than eighteen, I would think. It might be she worked there before they raised the drinking age. I remember going to the bar one night to try to help her and the boyfriend reconcile after a fight, but with no luck. They broke up permanently

So, yes, perhaps all the moving did contribute to Sebastian's and the other children's problems. Still, the closest I come to understanding, the closest I come to a key, is to remember my two children from their infant years. I look at Sebastian and I see my first wife. He loves cooking; she loves cooking. He is really into his children although he is on the road a lot; she is really into family, children, and grandchildren.

The first key—I think almost any parent who thinks about it will agree—is in the genes. It's genetic. It's blood. We are, to a larger extent than we want to admit, programmed. Such a view goes against the optimistic American faith that we are in control of our own destinies. Of course, how we are brought up plays a significant role. That's a second key. Courtney's first husband comes from French Catholic Cajun parents, New Orleans people who moved west to El Paso to work on the railroads. They were hard drinking, hard smoking, and hard partying people, and my stepchildren may have acquired their behaviors from the father's paternal traditions and genes.

People tell me the older I get, the more I'm like my father when he was this age. I wish I'd known my father better at this age to see how this gene business plays out; unfortunately, we were living in different parts of the country by then—he in upstate New York, I in Texas. Yes, the genes are the closest I come to a key. We are programmed. Identical twins separated at birth are often found to be working the same jobs and to be fond of the same brand of beer and cigarettes. Recently, a gene was reportedly discovered in some men that makes them more likely to have extramarital affairs.

That last piece of research seems culturally biased to me. Have they run the same genetic studies on women?

55

Now, as to why my son Sebastian got into drugs—was it my fault? Yes. Was it his fault? Yes. Was it my second wife, Courtney, and her children's fault? Yes. Was it my first wife's fault? Yes. Was it existential? Maybe.

What can be accomplished at this late stage by pointing fingers or attempting to assess blame? Doing so won't turn back the clock and undo what happened. I do it only in the hope it might benefit parents reading this book or a son or daughter reading that is addicted to a debilitating drug. Looking at complex interrelated causes might help to lead to recovery and cure.

I know I carry the pain of this experience in my soul at all times. Others may be put together differently, but the pain and guilt I suffer over my son has made it

> **My son is never far from my thoughts. I suffer because I imagine him suffering.**

hard to get up in the morning and grind through the days of work necessary to earn a living. My son is never far from my thoughts. I suffer because I imagine him suffering, and that may be the reason I chose to call my boy Sebastian here in these pages. Of course I do not use his real name.

Many of us have seen Saint Sebastian in paintings, his body riddled with arrows, twisting in pain. That old image is a powerful one—in a way perfect for representing all those addicted to dangerous drugs, and of course it is the child's suffering that makes the parent suffer. To get up and get going every day, to lift above our suffering—that may be why some of us grind up coffee. We need to get ourselves jump-started by an energetic jolt of the mildly addictive coffee bean. Maybe the great and happy poet Walt Whitman didn't carry the pain, or maybe he invented his generous and joyful literary persona because he knew deeply the pain and wanted to help those of us struggling to carry the weight.

All I know is that I carry the pain, and I know my son Sebastian carries it, and God can't be a permanent cure. My guess is suffering is ongoing, built into the flow of existence, because existence always requires struggle, sacrifice, hope, love, and loss. God as a personal therapist may ease things but can't do away with realities that stare us daily in the face.

Perhaps for Christians, Jesus' death depicted in art on the cross symbolizes and acknowledges suffering. Jesus had to suffer great physical pain, and so we suffer also, in a lesser way, psychologically and perhaps physically. Pardon my preaching here, but let me admit to being a quiet fan of Jesus. As the rock song goes, "Jesus is just all right with me."

Let me also apologize to those reading who aren't comfortable with Jesus talk. I grew up, in part, in the Unitarian Universalist Church, and with that heritage it's also possible to say, "Buddha is just all right with me," or "Krishna is just all right with me." The American writer Jack Kerouac said in an interview that Christ and Buddha are the same. Many are unaware of the Universalist in Unitarianism, its acknowledgment of more than one path to the light and its belief that all creatures finally gain salvation. No one remains forever in hell. To me, all spiritual teachings remain different languages aimed at the same goal: a celebration of the tenuous miracles of life and a celebration of the robust and grand ongoing creation. All the rest is dangerous mythological nonsense, attempts by the powerful to control the weak. I was taught in the Oak Park Unitarian Universalist Church I attended with my mother that Jesus was not solely the biological son of God. As the son of Mary also, he was human—not divine—but, by his teaching and actions, he proved to be one of the greatest humans who ever lived. Even the medieval Catholic theologian Peter Abelard taught that what we got from Jesus was a pattern of how to be a good person and how both to endure suffering and achieve resurrection. From such teachings I've surmised that Christ is, among many other things, the patron saint of the unwanted.

I'm sure Jesus' father, Joseph, was profoundly confused, indeed irritated, and not consoled one bit that the "other man" was supposedly divine who impregnated his future wife non-physically, using a spermatic ray gun, to maintain her virginity. Back then, of course, they did not know about a woman's eggs or about Mary's contributions to the genetic makeup of Jesus. They believed the sperm contained homunculi, tiny complete humans invisible to the eye. The woman's womb was merely an oven where the bread of the baby rose until it was big enough and strong enough to survive outside the woman's body.

I wonder if, in the history of humankind, most children have been unwanted and if it is the unwanted who suffer this pain most intimately. Orphans—the most unwanted it seems—have the highest risk for mental illness. For much of the human race throughout history, it's been a hardscrabble battle to survive. Much of the earth's populations remain poor peasants or urban proletariat living hand-to-mouth, dependent on the weather for food and survival. Children are at first a burden—another mouth to feed—and only become a blessing when they become old enough and strong enough to work the fields and raise crops, sail the seas and catch fish, or find a job.

I can usually sense in a month after meeting a person if they were wanted at birth or not. Being unwanted, I think, is the third key that explains why my son Sebastian got lost for so many years in drugs. I was unwanted; he was unwanted. To put it in biblical terms, the sins of the fathers were visited upon the sons. I quibble with the term "sin" here, since no child chooses to be unwanted. Perhaps "unwantedness" is what the old theologians had in the back of their minds when they came up with the notion of "original sin," the sin we are born with, that comes with being human, bound to the process of birth and death in families.

The renowned author and long time heroin addict William Burroughs said in an interview in *The Job*: "Everyone seems to consider that parents have every right to inflict on their children any sort of pernicious nonsense from which they themselves suffer, and which was passed on to them in turn by their parents, so that the whole human race is crippled in childhood, and this is done by the family."

I could have called this book "The Unwanted," and made Jesus muse and patron saint of the unwanted. It is Jesus who says in Mathew 19:30, "But many who are first will be last, and the last, first."

56

In the conservative college town I live in now, I don't run into as many of the unwanted as I used to. The young I meet tend to be from economically secure upper middle class families where the children are few and deeply loved. Families can be as much and even more about giving love than about crippling children. This town is in a way encouraging about the human prospect and about family, but the place also makes me feel out of place. Insecurity and alienation are more natural to me. Happiness breeds complacency, and complacency breeds boredom. It is the unwanted, the sufferers, who seem to me to have the brightest light around the body:

> *The suffering you sing from*
> *draws you toward completeness.*
> *Your faultless grief*
> *that cries in need*
> *is the blessed key.*
> *Listen to the dog's moaning for its master.*
> *Such crooning is what unites.*
> *So many faithful muts,*
> *yet we do not know their names.*
> *Teach your soul*
> *to love like a crooning dog.*
> —Rumi (a rendering)

I began by describing the process of writing this book with a golf metaphor, the poor golfer hacking and whacking away. I've made it down the course as if by magic through these fifty-some small strokes or sections. Being unwanted can be a kind of blessing. It can lead you to connect with the poor, the put-down, and the losers; it can develop your compassion for others, and compassion is the greatest of blessings, more crucial than pure good looks or intelligence. From compassion comes light.

At the beginning of this book I wandered off into a defense of Venezuelan president Hugo Chavez. I often think of what the filmmaker Orson Welles said, "Ye gods, stand up for mavericks!"

57

So I carry this pain and need all the distraction our gorgeous world throws in our direction: roadside carnivals you pass on the freeway but don't have time to stop and enjoy (I do at least enjoy the turning of the colored lights), birdsong, green grass, the flowering crepe myrtle even in the heat of a rainless summer when I take my dog for a walk, my family greeting me when I get home from a day of work, my daughter Ariel thanking me for taking her in the car to buy a dress or to visit a friend, my wife Sayuri's brilliant and wise insights and her gourmet Japanese cooking, and of course my old friend, the good grey poet Walt Whitman.

If drugs could cure this suffering of the soul, if, when I was young and naïve, somebody had offered me drugs, I would have hoped, without knowing, that the drug was for far more than kicks, was for more than even seeing God as some claim to have done on LSD and even cocaine.

> **We know from the published letters of Mother Teresa how even she suffered.**

The drugs, I would have hoped, could cure the soul's suffering. We are looking for a less painful way to make the light. The psychoanalyst Carl Jung once said of alcohol, "Why do you think they call it spirits?" Yes, if drugs had been as readily available in my youth as they were so available in Sebastian's early years, I might certainly have tried them.

But drugs do not end suffering. All they can do is numb the

pain a while. William Burroughs, the addict writer, described heroin as staring at your shoe all day, and then you become a slave trying to pay for the habit of shoe staring. A philosophy professor I know works with addicts; he does so because he is himself a twenty-some-year recovering alcoholic. He tells me of women and men who lose their teeth, put on thirty years, and sell their homes to maintain their methamphetamine habits—some in a period of less than eight months.

The longer you use certain addictive drugs, the more you have to take in order to get the numbing feeling that first relieves the suffering and then makes you feel zombie dead.

Nearly everybody I know has got the pain, but of course they don't talk about it. In America, suffering—originally a recognized and even honored religious experience—seems now to be viewed as a personality deficiency. "Pack up your troubles in an old kit bag and smile, smile, smile." We're supposed to always appear perky and positive, to think on the bright side, and, no doubt, a positive attitude at times can be beneficial. America, however, seems to have abandoned realism, as Barbara Ehrenreich argues in her 2009 book *Bright Sided: How the Relentless Promotion of Positive Thinking Has Undermined America*.

I have known a few who seemed so focused on others they either didn't appear to have the pain or didn't notice it, but they're extremely rare. We know from the published letters of Mother Teresa how even she suffered. I like to be around these givers; they can make you laugh and teach by example how to do as they do. But still the pain lingers and simmers. Not always. Pure happy days surprise us. I had such a day last week, typing up a manuscript I've been writing about cats. My back and neck began to hurt after a couple of hours at the keyboard, but that is not the suffering I'm talking about. When you get quiet and the world grows silent—say, when you first lay down at night in bed—there it is, that anxious-ness, that American loneliness, that pain. It is at that moment I say, "Thank you for the gift of this day."

Perhaps you are lucky, reader. Perhaps church attendance or inspiring sermons keep you on the straight and narrow, or maybe you're busy focused on outward things, loving and giving acts, so you don't get singed so much by the suffering. I hope that old age, all the years of suffering, have made me more generous. I appreciate Sebastian more. I understand my son Parker and his sufferings and difficulties. He, too, faced terrible challenges as a child, and his path as a musician is not an easy one.

But Sebastian and I are silent on the meaningful, deep things and are not able to talk over our painful history or even discuss suffering. But life is long, and who knows what may come later, when we're both older and wiser.

I know about our silence—my silence—the frozen block of the soul inside, for I've been fighting that freeze all my life, and it is what made me a writer. That's the last key, I believe, the last door to be unlocked that contains the final chapter of explanation about what happened to Sebastian.

"What we have here, gentlemen, is a failure of communication."

Those words are spoken in a church in the final climatic scene of *Cool Hand Luke* (1967) by Paul Newman's character, Luke.

Right now I enjoy immensely Sebastian's long telephone calls, his generous wife, our visits together, and his four children—with personalities from shy to rambunctious—out of two of his three marriages. Sebastian, by love or luck or by some basic instinct for survival, heroically came through the darkness. He found a stable relationship; he found work that paid decently and did not

Sebastian found his own solution to drugs gradually and thus saved himself.

stress him out too much. Trucking indeed meets his need for solitude. He does not want to go to jail again, so he submits to the drug tests on the job and pays his child support. All the adolescent concepts of idiotic coolness, picked up from friends or from the media, seem purged from his body. Raising a family, being a father, has filled the holes in his soul that he used to try to fill with drugs. Family has given him purpose and meaning. Rather than looking for keys, it's better to focus on the miracle that is the change in his life, that is his resurrection. For us it is as if he has come back from the dead.

And so I live on hope. To all the parents out there suffering with troubled sons and daughters, please maintain and continue to live with hope. I pray and keep my fingers crossed. I hope you pray and keep your fingers crossed. Jim Morrison, the troubled lead singer for the rock-and-roll band the Doors didn't mean it this way in his song, and did not break on through himself until his death, but Sebastian, my lovely son, my dear boy, seems to have broken through—mysteriously, miraculously—to another, better side. I hope the same happens for other parents and their drug-troubled children.

It's possible!

And am I not a father blessed?

Sebastian found his own solution to drugs gradually and thus saved himself. Psychologists didn't solve his problem. His parents couldn't solve his problem. AA and NA didn't solve his problem. What happened seems a miracle. Over the years he worked things out gradually, following his instincts, becoming a family man.

And now, if he could only quit smoking.

He tells me he's working on it.

Dr. Charles Taylor has taught university classes for over thirty years in Texas, New Mexico, and Illinois. After undergoing trans-actional analysis, he studied the role literature and writing might play in the processes of healing, not only for the writer but also for the reader. He then focused many creative writing workshops upon writers dealing with their own personal "knots" (as he calls them) and using their creativity in writing to begin the work of untying. He has served on the Board of Directors of the Poetry Therapy Institute and helped develop ways to use poetry as a key to under-standing in order to facilitate healing. For more than two decades he has taught in the English department at Texas A&M University, serving for several years as the Coordinator of Creative Writing. He has also worked in prisons and in other special needs pro-grams. His publications include novels, nonfiction, and poetry. He is married to Takako Saito. They have three children.

As promised earlier in the book, here are some blank pages for notes:

For your notes:

For your notes:

Breinigsville, PA USA
26 January 2011
254176BV00001B/3/P